THE ISLANDS OF BAHRAIN

An Illustrated Guide to their Heritage

by

Angela Clarke

The Bahrain Historical & Archaeological Society

1981

TRIBUTE

Dr. Abdul Latif Kanoo
President

Bahrain Historical & Archaeological Society

joins his fellow members in congratulating the

Society's Patron

His Highness Shaikh Isa bin Sulman Al-Khalifa

on the occasions of the

20th Anniversary of his Accession Ceremony
16th December 1961

and the

10th Anniversary of Bahrain's Declaration of Independence
15th August 1971

HH Shaikh Isa bin Sulman Al-Khalifa,
Amir of Bahrain

Bahrain Historical & Archaeological Society
P.O. Box 5087
Manama
Bahrain
Arabian Gulf

First published 1981

Production and Printing - **Modern Graphics,** Manama, Bahrain

ACKNOWLEDGEMENTS

The Bahrain Historical and Archaeological Society is indebted to the following institutions of Bahrain for their generous financial assistance and support of this publication.

Ministry of Information
Bank of Bahrain & Kuwait
Bahrain Petroleum Company B.S.C. (Closed)
Gulf International Bank B.S.C.
National Bank of Bahrain
Al Bahrain Arab African Bank (E.C.) - "ALBAAB"
British Bank of the Middle East
Banque de L'Indochine et de Suez
Grindlays Bank Limited
Chartered Bank Limited
The Saudi National Commercial Bank
Chemical Bank
Bahrain Financing Company
Algemene Bank Nederland
American Express International Banking Corporation
B.A.I.I. (Middle East) E.C.
Citibank N.A.
Credit Suisse
Aluminium Bahrain - "ALBA"
Trans-Arabian Investment Bank E.C. "TAIB"
Continental Illinois National Bank and Trust Company of Chicago
Manufacturers Hanover Trust Co.
Banque de Paris et des Pays-Bas
Thomas Cook Travellers Cheques Limited
Security Pacific National Bank
Bankers Trust Company
Banque Nationale de Paris
Halliburton Limited
Irving Trust Company
Lloyds Bank International Limited
Merrill Lynch International & Co.
Scandinavian Bank Limited
Arab Latin American Bank - Arlabank
Brown & Root S.A.
European Arab Bank (Middle East) E.C.
Kleinwort Benson (Middle East) E.C.
DHL International Courier Services

STATE OF BAHRAIN
MINISTRY OF INFORMATION
OFFICE OF THE MINISTER

الرقـم :

التاريخ :

No.

Date November 15th. 1981

The President
Bahrain Historical & Archeological Society
State of Bahrain.

I am pleased to write to you on the occasion of the publication,
THE ISLANDS OF BAHRAIN, An Illustrated Guide to their Heritage.
I am impressed by the amount of information and details which
the author has covered in a systematic and interesting style.
This book is a valuable edition to the literature available on
Bahrain's history and culture.

Your Society has done a great deal to encourage consciousness
amongst Bahrainis of their historical and archeological heritage,
and to organize the endeavours of interested expatriates living
in Bahrain to contribute their knowledge and personal efforts
in this direction. Your members should be proud of your extensive
programmes of lectures, tours of historical sites and excavation
activities.

This book represents the best example of your society's contribution to our programme to explore and preserve our national
heritage.

Yours Sincerely,

Tariq Almoayed
Minister of Information.

P. O. Box 253
Telex : 8399 GJ

ص . ب : ٢٥٣
تلكس ، ٨٣٩٩ جي. ج

FOREWORD

The Bahrain Historical and Archaeological Society is pleased to present this guidebook to Bahrain in commemoration of the twentieth anniversary of the accession of His Highness the Amir, Shaikh Isa bin Sulman Al-Khalifa, whom we are honoured to have as our patron. It is our hope that this guidebook will fulfill one of the Society's pledged objectives, that is the encouragement of the study and awareness of the history, archaeology and traditions of Bahrain and the Gulf region, and that it will thus be a source of interest and information both to Bahrainis and to their visitors.

The executive committee of the Society is privileged to take this opportunity of congratulating His Highness the Amir. It wishes to express its considerable gratitude to the author for her tireless efforts and to the various Ministries, institutions and individuals who have given their support and assistance in completion of this guidebook.

AUTHOR'S ACKNOWLEDGEMENTS

The timely completion of this guidebook would not have been possible without the generous guidance and facilities which have been granted to the author, often at short notice.

I am indebted to the following individuals and organisations for their significant contributions to the project: Abdulrahman Musameh (Superintendent), Bahrain Museum, Ahmed Alarifi (Superintendent), Directorate of Culture and Arts, Dr. Abdul Latif Kanoo (President) BHAS, Dr. Mohd. Al-Khosai (Director of Culture and Arts) Ministry of Information, Shaikha Haya Al-Khalifa (Director of Museums and Archaeology) Ministry of Information, Dr. J.E. Curtis (Assistant Keeper) Department of Western Asiatic Antiquities, British Museum, London, John Ruffle, Gulbenkian Museum of Oriental Arts, Durham, England, Professor Peter Warren, Dept. of Classical Archaeology, University of Bristol, England, John R. Gourlay, Bahrain Petroleum Company B.S.C. (Closed), and Jean Williams (Librarian) BHAS, The Bank of Oman, Bahrain and Kuwait, Chemical Bank, Dai-ichi Kangyo Bank and Falcon Cinefoto.

Especially I should like to thank Jeanne Cassin and Jean Hirst for their critical appraisal of the text, Ruth Murley for typing the manuscript, Michael McKinlay for his unfailing encouragement, Joan Porter for her untiring assistance and Andy Chen for his technical guidance.

To all these people and organisations I extend my sincere gratitude.

CONTENTS

PART III: LOCATION GUIDE

Sh. Hamed Causeway
Abu Mahur Fort
Sh. Isa's House
Siyadi House
Sh. Salman's House

The Bahrain Museum
Bahrain International Airport
Umm Al-Khayleh Spring
Sh. Daij bin Hamed's Summer Palace
Siyadi Country House
Halat An-Naim
Halat As-Sulatah
Hidd
Arad Fort
Coastguard Base
Abu Mahur Fort

Masjid Ras Rummaan
British Embassy
British Council
Adviserate
Manama Centre
Government House
Friday Mosque
Almoayyed Buildings
National Bank of Bahrain
Bait Skinner
British Bank of the Middle East
The Old Law Courts
Yateem Centre
Former long-distance dhow harbour
Old Pier Site
First Petrol Filling Station
Bab Al-Bahrain

Site of Old Customs Square and Pier
Wednesday Market
Pearl Cinema
Central Market
Mina Manama
Chamber of Commerce Building
Ministry of Finance and Foreign Affairs
Gulf International Bank New Building
Ministry of Justice and Islamic Affairs
Bahrain Monetary Agency
Kuwait Embassy
Bait Al-Koran

Abu Mahur Fort
Gudaibiya Palace (Guest Palace)
Juffair Sports Dome
Al-Khalifa Family former summer residences
Mina Sulman
Sitra Causeway
Nabih Salih
Sitra
Tank Farm
Refinery
Fish Traps
Manama Palace
Wind Tower

Al-Awadiyah Conservation Area
Ga'wa
Arab Bakery
Qalaat Al-Diwan (Manama Fort)
Water Gardens
Suq Al-Khamis Mosque
Thursday Market (Suq Al-Khamis) Site
Bilad Al-Qadim site
Isa Town
Aali Pottery
Nura (lime) kilns - Aali
Royal Mounds - Aali

University College
Television Station
Directorate of Arts and Culture
Gulf Polytechnic
Adhari Pool

West Rifaa (Rifaa Al-Gharbi)
Old Racecourse
Awali
New Racecourse
Hoopoe Bird Well-Head
Sakhir Palace
Arabian Gulf University Site
Dar Khulaib Qanat System
BANAGAS Plant
Tropospheric Scatter Station
First Oil Well
Jebel Camp site
Al-Gosaibi's House
Hanaini Spring
Rifaa Fort
East Rifaa (Rifaa Ash-Sharqi)

Jasra
Hamala
Dumistan
Karzakkan
Al-Malikiyah
Dar Khulaib Qanat System
West Rifaa and Saar Tumuli

Dhow Builders' Yard
Jidhafs
Karbabad Basket Makers
Qalaat Al-Bahrain (Bahrain Fort)
Al-Migsha'a
Barbar Temple

Diraz Temple
Ain Umm Es-Sujur
Experimental Gardens
Budaiya
Qanat System
Bani Jamra Fabric Weavers
Al-Hajjar Site

PART IV: AIDS AND SUPPLEMENTS

Bahrain Historical and Archaeological Society
Committee for Arabian and Gulf Studies
Excavations Conducted in Bahrain

Abbreviations
Bibliography
Chronology
Glossary
Site Index

PLATES

FRONT COVER -   Sakhir Palace,   Engelbert   Kraxnester
                Mosque at Sunset

COLOUR PHOTO-   Nabih Salih island   Engelbert   Kraxnester
      GRAPHS -

                Gudaibiya Palace   Engelbert   Kraxnester

                Arad Fort   Engelbert   Kraxnester

                Muhamedia Island   Engelbert   Kraxnester

                Qalaat Al-Bahrain   Ministry of Informa-
                aerial shot   tion

                Mina Manama   Author

BLACK & WHITE PHOTOGRAPHS -

BAPCO Bahrain   Plates 3, 5, 6, 7, 8, 9, 15, 16, 17, 21, 25, 80, 81, 87, 88, 91, 92, 93, 94, 95, 96, 97, 105, 115, 116

Falcon Cinefoto Bahrain   Plates 2, 19, 23, 24, 33, 35, 37, 39, 40, 43, 47, 48, 49, 50, 51, 53, 61, 64, 70, 82, 83, 106, 113, 118, 119, 121

Quartet Books, London   Plates 20, 55, 56, 57, 58, 59

Trustees of the British Museum   Plate 10

Bahrain Historical & Archaeological Society   Plates 11, 12, 68, 125

Bahrain Museum   Plates 31, 32, 34, 79

Dr. W.J. Donaldson, Outspan Organisation, London   Plate 60

Namara Publications, London   Plate 62

Dr. Abdul Latif Kanoo   Plate 100

Photographs not listed above were taken by the author.

DRAWINGS/FIGURES

The following diagrams are reproduced by courtesy of :

Geo Abstracts Ltd., University of East Anglia, Norwich, U.K.	Figs. 1, 2
Bahrain Historical & Archaeological Society	Figs. 3, 15, 20, 21, 22, 25
Serge Cleuziou, Centre de Recherches Archeologiques, Paris, France	Fig. 4
Seton Lloyd, Archaeology of Mesopotamia, Thames & Hudson	Fig. 5
Pelican Books, London	Figs. 6, 7, 8, 9, 10
G.R.H. Wright, The Old Amiri Palace, Doha, Qatar National Museum	Figs. 11, 12
El-Said, Geometric Concepts in Islamic Art, World of Islam Festival Publishing Co. UK	Fig. 13
Fuad Khuri, Tribe and State in Bahrain University of Chicago Press	Fig. 14
Mehdi Bahadori, Scientific American Vol. 238, Feb. 1978	Fig. 17
Penguin Books, London	Fig. 16
A.D.P.F. Paris	Figs. 18, 19
U.N'E'S'O.	Figs. 23, 24

MAPS

Major Excavation Sites in Bahrain - Drawn by Jean-Paul
                                    Boulanger, a member
                                    of J.F. Salles' French
                                    Archaeological Mission
                                    to Janussan, 1981.

The remaining were drawn by **Modern Graphics**.

HOW THE GUIDE WORKS

The Guide is divided into two independent, yet complementary sections, each designed to fulfill diverse reader requirements. Emphasis is placed on the visual characteristics of
the archaeology, architecture and traditional skills of Bahrain.

A background perspective precedes these sections, while the
final component supplements the range of this handbook with
selected appendices and suggestions for further reading.
Data such as embassies, hotels and travel agents is not included as it is readily available.

PART I: BACKGROUND PERSPECTIVE

In order to appreciate fully Parts II and III, a background perspective of the islands is recommended. This is the function of
Part I.

It should be noted that this is not definitive as a documentary
study would create an imbalance in the visual concept of the
guide. Readers seeking a more scholarly approach may refer
to the bibliography at the back of the book.

PART II: THEMATIC GUIDE

Perhaps your preference is for Paleolithic flint sites or industrial archaeology, barasti (palm frond) houses or fort
construction, dhow building or gold-thread embroidery? Part
II will guide you to your choice of reading as it is designed for
those:

- with interest in specific subjects only
- unable to tour the sites
- requiring an outline of the potential before selecting a trip.

Each theme is sub-divided into categories which are summarised to the extent of shared characteristics, including a resume
of known sites. For reference, features no longer extant will
be identified on the relevant maps included in this section.
As a rule they will not appear in the location guide (Part III)
since this is intended for visitors to existing places of interest.

PART III: LOCATION GUIDE

The islands of Bahrain have been segmented into gridded sections which form individual routes from which the traveller can make a selection. Each excursion comprises a map, identifying the landmarks within it, accompanied by individual site profiles.

PART IV: AIDS & SUPPLEMENTS

This final component comprises a chronology, glossary and site index as aids to the guide, together with supplements to its range in the form of listed summaries and a bibliography.

NOTE ON TRANSLITERATION

Most Arabic linguists would agree on one point. Their language is a complex discipline, subject to wide interpretation and a lifetime of study. Usage varies greatly among the Arabic-speaking nations of Africa, Arabia, the Middle and Near East. Even within the Arabian Peninsula, where the language is colloquially known as Gulf Arabic, there are many variations in dialect and spelling. Bringing the focus to Bahrain does not resolve the matter.

As there is no authoritative ruling on the subject, few Arabic-speakers would be bold enough to suggest their fellows' choice of usage is wrong, yet they may prefer an equally plausible alternative. Therefore, Arabic transliteration generally used in Bahrain today appears in this guide. Readers who may be familiar with other spelling choices may refer to the glossary which cross-references certain variations.

INTRODUCTION

Bahrain, like many developing countries in the Middle East, has changed with great speed during the last quarter of a century. Much of this is hidden advance; commercial expertise, educational opportunities, health improvement, technological development and so on. The opposite facet is the visual impact of environmental change; land reclamation, building schemes, communications networks, industrialisation. All are vital to a thriving 20th century economy.

But achieving progress is bound to evoke conflict between conservationists and town planners bidding to modernise. Often a compromise is reached which will reflect society's willingness to accept that there is more than one perspective to the subject of restoration versus renewal.

It is not the purpose of this guide to join the debate. But there is a significant point to remember when assessing such sensitivities. Decisions made today, for whatever reason, will take their place in history tomorrow. Simultaneously, deeds will transform some of our visual horizons irrevocably. Future generations will judge whether such action was of long-term value to the community. Inevitably, from the benefit of hindsight, there will be successes and errors.

The burden of achieving the right balance is immense, as is demonstrated in Bahrain. Bronze Age enthusiasts will defend the rescue of the threatened burial mounds. Enlightened economists will argue that the loss of an estimated five hundred of the many thousand tumuli to the proposed new town and the Bahrain-Saudi Arabia Causeway (themselves future monuments) is little sacrifice for the sake of the nation's future prosperity. It is in this context of complementary change that this guide to the Islands of Bahrain has been written, highlighting the endowment of a rich heritage, yet acknowledging the essential role which modern events play in the continuation of its quality.

ISLANDS OF BAHRAIN -

Topography prior to commencement of land reclamation and causeway building 50 years ago. (c. 1931)

SAUDI ARABIA

MUHARRAQ

MANAMA

JIDDA

NABIH SALIH

SITRA

UMM AN-NASSAN

AALI ISA TOWN

RIFAA AL-GHARBI

RIFAA ASH SHARQI

AWALI

JEBEL DUKHAN

BAHRAIN

NORTH

Bahrain's Islands

Cultivation

Burial Mounds

SAUDI ARABIA

HOWAR ISLANDS

HOWAR

QATAR

SCALE: KILOMETRES 5

MILES 5

PART 1: BACKGROUND PERSPECTIVE

1. TOPOGRAPHY OF THE ARCHIPELAGO

People arriving in Bahrain for the first time, especially at night, could be forgiven the thought that they have landed upon a single-island state. The drive from the airport to Manama, the capital, belies the fact that the traveller crosses a causeway linking one island (Muharraq) to another (Bahrain).

More than forty years ago, it was another story. A launch took passengers across the deep channel where, upon reaching shallow water, they were required to transfer to a skiff. This then took them to a short stone pier for disembarkation. But before this was built in 1901 crossings had ended less elegantly. It was a matter of paddling or being carried ashore.

BAHRAIN, meaning two seas, is an archipelago of thirty-three small islands located mid-way down the Arabian Gulf. One suggestion is that the name is attributed to the Archipelago's position approximately 24 kilometres east of Saudi Arabia's sea-board and a little further from the north-west coast of the peninsular State of Qatar. Another theory refers to the incidence of fresh water rising in the form of numerous springs beneath the islands' surface and the offshore sea-bed. The total land area is about 410 square kilometres, which for the most part is surfaced with hard barren limestone rock, covered in many places with sand.

There are six principal islands in the group, the largest being Bahrain from which the State takes its name. It measures approximately 44 x 17 kilometres with the southernmost point terminating at the headland, Ras al-Barr. Rocky slopes dip downwards and outwards from the rim of a centrally located erosion basin to disappear into the remarkably shallow sea and coral reefs around the island, or under the sandy beaches. This central basin of about 20 x 7 kilometres is outlined by cliffs which form an almost continuous ridge around it, varying in height from 6 to 30 metres. In the centre are relatively high peaks, the highest of which is the Jebel Dukhan, Mountain of Smoke.

Plate 1: West Rifaa (foreground) Awali (middle-distance) Jebel Dukhan (horizon)

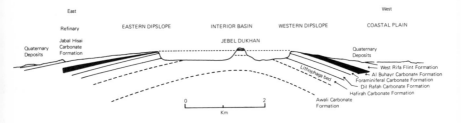

Fig. 1: Diagrammatic east-west geological section through the centre of Bahrain island.

This derives its name from haze formations which cause the rocks to assume an aura of grey smoke rising from the desert, particularly evident in the summer heat and humidity. Although by most geological standards, a height of 122.4 metres (445 ft.) would rate no more than a hill, this mysterious Mountain of Smoke provides an ample evening look-out for sighting the gas flares of Dukhan (Qatar) and Dhahran (Saudi Arabia) some 40 or more kilometres away.

A causeway and swing-bridge, completed in 1942, linked Bahrain to Muharraq island. However, as sail gave way to diesel-power, the need for high-masted dhows to pass through the deep-water channel to Muharraq Port ended, and so the swing-bridge became obsolete. Now, a four-lane highway crosses this sector, although plans to widen this to six lanes were announced in 1981.

Plate 2: 'Boom' under sail

Plate 3: Muharraq Swing-bridge

MUHARRAQ forms the northern part of the island group. As it is low-lying and susceptible to flooding at high-tide, airport and road traffic were frequently immobilised. However, subsequent land reclamation and raised roads have helped to alleviate the problem.

Two smaller islands lie to the south-east of Muharraq, **UMM ASH-SHAGAR** and **UMM ASH-SHUJAIRA**. Originally fishermen were the sole inhabitants, living in stone and barasti houses, but now a causeway links the islets to 300,000 square metres of reclaimed land, the site of Bahrain's dry-dock complex.

Nestling to the south of Muharraq's Arad peninsula are four other islets **HALAT AS-SULATAH**, **HALAT AL-KHULAIFAT HALAT AN-NAIM** and **ABU MAHUR**. Although none of these boast an area of more than a few hundred square metres they support domestic, religious and military architecture which some observers consider would have been fine examples of their type at the time of their construction.

Plate 4: Halat As-Sulatah

Taking a course down the east coast of Bahrain island, visitors by launch or sailing boat will encounter Khor al-Kabb, a large bay sheltering the island of **NABIH SALIH**. Its two main springs, Ain as-Safahiyan and Ain al-Khadra, provide natural bathing pools, as well as irrigation for thick cultivation. Sea-borne pilgrims paying their respects to the tomb of Salih, after whom the island is named, will find ample shade under its date palms. However, motorists can now reach Nabih Salih by means of a small bridge, which links it to the Bahrain-Sitra Causeway completed in 1977.

SITRA, south-east of Nabih Salih and close to the coast of Bahrain, has become an industrial complex, housing amongst other enterprises Bahrain Petroleum Company's "Tank Farm" and a new power station.

Fifty years ago Sitra island was isolated from Bahrain, relying on its pools and gardens to support the village inhabitants. However, with the advent of oil being struck in 1932, a bridge was built by BAPCO from Sitra's west coast to Bahrain's east coast so that the company's equipment could be brought over-land from the Sitra jetty to their Jebel camp. When the deep water channel near this jetty became a strategic and busy shipping lane, it became necessary to link Sitra's north coast to the newly established Port of Mina Sulman on Bahrain island, hence the 3-kilometre Bahrain-Sitra Causeway.

Plate 5: Building the Sitra Bridge 1930s

JIDDA is a small, rocky island about 5 kilometres to the north-west of Bahrain. Unlike the other Bahrain islands, high yellowish-grey cliffs rise steeply from the sea, except for a level strip of land to the south which has been cultivated extensively into gardens growing date-palms, cork trees, pomegranates, oleanders and jasmine. The late Sir Charles Belgrave [1] commented in his memoirs that the island was "a great place for birds" and around it there was "first-rate fishing".

Of particular note are the stone quarries. These are believed to have supplied the Bronze Age tumuli builders with their slabs for grave construction, but more recently, an Arabic inscription carved into one of the cliffs reveals that in the month of Shaban 968 A.H. (that is April or May 1561 A.D.) [2] the 100,000th rock was cut for mending the towers of the Bahrain Fort (Qalaat Al-Bahrain). As Jidda is now Bahrain's long-term penal settlement, access to the island is restricted.

UMM AN-NASSAN to the south of Jidda is the second largest of the Bahrain islands. It is sandy and flat with the exception of two small limestone hills towards its centre in which a number of rock tombs have been fashioned. However, the tranquillity of the island, its date groves and a herd of black buck and gazelle, introduced by the late Shaikh Hamed, is about to be disturbed.

The signing of the Bahrain-Saudi Arabia Causeway Contract on 8th July 1981 heralds the beginning of unprecedented change for the State of Bahrain and particularly for this island. Not only is it destined to carry 3 kilometres of the new four-lane highway, serve as a customs and toll frontier, and provide a construction base for the contractors, but it is also to have a new island companion of reclaimed land, destined to house a vast cement plant for servicing the Bahrain sector of the 25-kilometre causeway.

1 - Sir Charles Belgrave - Adviser from 1926-1957 to Shaikh Hamed bin Isa Al-Khalifa (d. 1942) and Shaikh Sulman bin Hamed Al-Khalifa (d. 1961)

2 - A.H. (After Hijriya) Islamic Calendar based on sighting 12 annual lunar cycles.
A.D. (Anno Domini) Gregorian Calendar based on 365/6 days a year, hence the rotational variation of months.

THE HOWAR ISLANDS are the antithesis in every way to the hustle of the northern group of Bahrain's islands. They comprise sixteen closely-knit isles about 20 kilometres south-east of the southernmost headland of Bahrain, Ras al-Barr. Howar itself is the largest of the group being about 18 kilometres long and 1½ kilometres wide. The name was inspired by the notion that Howar (meaning young camel) looks like a miniature version of Bahrain island, its "mother", complete with a rocky outcrop in the centre, Al-Jebel. Settlement on the islands used to comprise two villages, a police post, and a mosque which provided shelter and solace for fishermen, the craftsmen who came to cut and "fire" gypsum and the occasional flint-site enthusiast.

As modern maps demonstrate, the Howar Group is closer to the Qatar peninsula than Bahrain island, a fact which has not been ignored by raiders and pirates. One such notable, Isa bin Tarif, who operated in the 19th century, used a long narrow shipping channel specially hewn out of the coral sea-bed, to serve as a passage to his fortress on the Qatar coast from where he sallied forth to attack vessels sailing around Bahrain's islands.

PRINCIPAL AINS (Springs) OF BAHRAIN

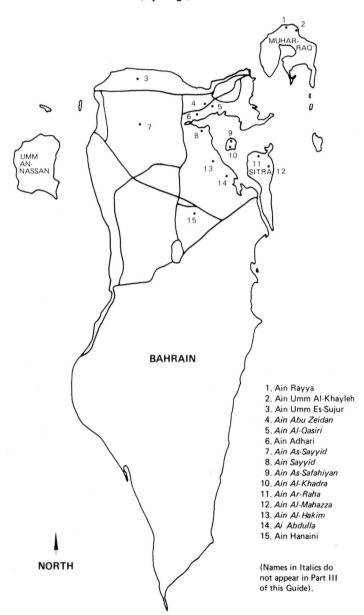

1. Ain Rayya
2. Ain Umm Al-Khayleh
3. Ain Umm Es-Sujur
4. *Ain Abu Zeidan*
5. *Ain Al-Qasiri*
6. Ain Adhari
7. *Ain As-Sayyid*
8. *Ain Sayyid*
9. *Ain As-Safahiyan*
10. *Ain Al-Khadra*
11. *Ain Ar-Raha*
12. *Ain Al-Mahazza*
13. *Ain Al-Hakim*
14. *Ai Abdulla*
15. Ain Hanaini

(Names in Italics do
not appear in Part III
of this Guide).

2. RESOURCES

WATER is arguably one of nature's few resources upon which mankind depends for survival, yet daily this liquid is taken for granted. In an age of technology, most of us will give scarcely a second thought to the prospect that water might not flow when we turn a tap, and even less to the notion that we might have to travel some way to fetch it.

Yet to the older residents of Bahrain this is no exaggeration. They can remember when drinking water was carried daily into the towns on the backs of donkeys and camels in skin water-bags (jirbeh), sometimes for journeys of 16 kilometres or more.

Theodore Bent writing in 1889 recalled that "those who can afford it send for water to a well, between Rufa'a Jebeli and Rufa'a Shergali (modern West Rifaa and East Rifaa), called *Hanaini*. Camels laden with skins may be seen coming into Manama every morning with this treasure". So one might ask quite reasonably, where did the water come from? There is no doubt that the pattern of settlement on Bahrain's islands owes its longevity to a rich endowment of natural springs, usually referred to as Ains. The fresh water supplying these is thought to have originated along the lines of limestone caverns, a ragged outline of which may be found around the Jebel Dukhan escarpment. Particularly stunning is a vast hollow which has been eroded by water, some 4.5 x 10.5 x 2m. at the head of a wadi facing the modern town of Awali. The remarkable patterns on its walls are presumed to be the work of nature and not man.

It is worth noting that Bahrain's central basin is considered at one time to have contained a large lake which probably existed from the Eocene to the Pleistocene period, a geological time-scale of millions of years ago. During very wet seasons shallow lakes still form in parts of the island which may account for seemingly inexplicable vegetation in the middle of the desert. The Tree of Life, a large thorn bush flourishing on the edge of what is believed to be a dried-up lagoon and the site of pre-Islamic settlements, is a fine example located towards the south of the island serving as a landmark for desert travellers.

In contrast, the impressive vegetation along the northern coast of Bahrain, and on Muharraq, Sitra and Nabih Salih islands, is almost entirely due to a number of fresh-water springs (ains) which prior to the drilling of artesian wells in the 1920s and 30s erupted as natural surface wells and as springs from within the lineal limits of the offshore reefs. The days are still within living memory when men went out in boats to the deep-water springs, dived down to the sea bed with leather water-skins, filled them at source, and then surfaced holding the mouth of the water-bag tightly closed. The water was then sold in the suq.

Bent recorded that "the town of Muharraq obtained its water supply from this curious sea-bed source, called *Biamahab*. At high tide when almost a fathom[1] of sea covered the spring, the water was brought up either by divers or by pushing a hollow bamboo down into it. At low tide women with large amphora[2] (two-handled storage jars) would wade out and fetch what water they required.

"The legend is that in the time of Murwan, a Chief of the Ibn Hakim from Qatif, wished to marry the lovely daughter of a Bahrain Chief. His suit was not acceptable so he made war on the islands and captured all the wells which supplied the towns on the bigger island, but the Guardian Deity of the Bahraini caused this spring to break out in the sea just before Muharraq and the invader was thus repulsed."

Among the most well-known ains are those which are located in the villages adjacent to the modern Shaikh Sulman Highway. Modern developments have obscured much of *Ain Al-Qasiri* which used to be a pleasure garden and picnic place not far from the Mosque Suq Al Khamis. *Ain Abu Zeidan* on the other hand, situated in the midst of the ruins of the islands' former capital, Bilad Al Qadim (Old Town), was reserved in the 19th century for the private use of the present Amir's great-grandfather, Shaikh Isa bin Ali Al-Khalifa, and his family. Subsequently a mosque was built over the spring.

1 - Fathom - A unit of length equal to 6 feet (1.828 metres) used for calculating depths of water.
2 - Local name baghleh.

Just a kilometre or so beyond the Mosque Suq Al-Khamis is a turning to the **Ain Adhari** (meaning Virgin's Pool). This in its time has supplied many kilometres of date groves through a canal of ancient workmanship. Nowadays a National Park surrounds the area, with the pool as its focal point where divers are said to be driven back by the force of the water gushing up from underground.

However, perhaps the most interesting ains are those which are less well known. **Ain Umm Es-Sujur** is located to the southeast of Diraz village adjacent to the Budaiya Highway. At the beginning of the Islamic era in the 7th century A.D. this was the largest of the three most important springs in Bahrain. Although the spring was filled in at a later date, recent excavation revealed a former holy shrine with unique statuary subjects on the well's steps.

The Chronicle of Al-Khalifa recalls that **Rayya** Palace (now demolished), called after a spring of that name on the north Muharraq coast, became a recreation resort for Shaikh Isa the First's family throughout the year. Samahidj Palace, near to Rayya Gardens and also demolished, was constructed in 1912 A.D. for Shaikh Isa's personal use. A contemporary house, now a research farm, was built near **Umm Al-Khayleh** (mother of young palm tree) spring.

Moving forward to the late 1920s, Charles Belgrave noted that "water from distant streams was sold in the Bazaar. At a higher price one could buy water from a well ten miles (16 kms.) off. An old water-carrier came daily with two tins of brackish water slung on a yoke across his shoulders. 'Fresh' drinking water was collected from the mail boats, which called at Bahrain once a fortnight. As there was no ice, we kept the water cool in porous earthenware jars".

Although in 1981 mains' water supplies much of Bahrain, any thought to dismiss these writers' observations as quaint antiquity should be tempered by the fact that village life depends on the ains almost as much today as it did a century ago. Occasionally one may see women walking to the springs near to their villages with large circular pans heaped with laundry, balanced perfectly on their heads. Bathing in the ains for hygiene as well as pleasure is still enjoyed by local men and

Plate 6 BAHREIN LAUNDRY
OCT. 25·34

boys, particularly in the Adhari Pool which remains a favourite meeting place; but perhaps the focus should end more appropriately on their economic role.

In the late 19th century there were about fifty villages scattered over the islands, recognisable from a distance by their patch of civilisation and groups of date palms. Except at Manama and Muharraq they had little or nothing to do with the pearl fisheries but with an exceedingly industrious race of people who cultivated the soil by means of irrigation from numerous wells. Worked like an Indian well by donkeys and bullocks on a running slope, buckets or skins for water descended as the animals ascended, and vice versa. There were generally three to six small wheels attached to a beam over which the ropes of as many leather buckets passed. When these buckets rose full, they tilted themselves over and the contents were taken by little channels to a reservoir which fed the dykes.

For those who take the trouble to wander through the countryside today, perhaps lured by the rhythmic sound of a motor, they will find the agricultural scene little changed from Bent's nineteenth century observations. Whilst diesel pumps have replaced the animals and buckets, farmers still employ networks of irrigation channels, systematically dammed with piles of cloths which divert the water's course according to requirements.

Even in the areas associated less with agriculture, the springs still perform a vital daily function. A notable example is the Amir's nursery garden which supplies trees and shrubs to the Municipality. This is irrigated by the *Hanaini* well near West Rifaa (see Route 6), which still produces some of the islands' purest water.

Plate 7:
Fred Davies and
William Taylor

OIL took its active industrial place in Bahrain just half a century ago with a momentous discovery by geologist Fred A. Davies. On the 14th May 1930 he stepped ashore on Bahrain with William F. Taylor, General Superintendent of the Standard Oil Company of California's Foreign Division. Greeted by Major Frank Holmes, the first chief local representative of SOCAL's newly-incorporated subsidiary Bahrain Petroleum Company (BAPCO), he set about his task of determining whether Bahrain should be drilled for oil.

Holmes, a New Zealand engineer, had been convinced of this for over a decade. "More than 20 years before the wealth of Kuwait and Saudi Arabia began to flow (c. 1918 A.D.), Holmes wrote to his wife:

'I personally believe that there will be developed an immense oil-field running from Kuwait right down the mainland coast.'

He was proved to be right. Nor did it take Davies long to conclude that Bahrain should be developed, although he warned that it could not be considered a first-class wildcat prospect. Davies walked the entire rim-rock of the Jebel Dukhan, spotted his site, and promptly built a cairn of stones siting the position for the first well.

Fred Davies standing beside
the Cairn of stones
which marked the site of
the first oil-well in Bahrain

Plate 8

Later, drillers swore that he had chosen the only place on the whole island that never had a breeze, but as it turned out this inconvenience was overwhelmed by the remarkable discovery that Davies, using few instruments to guide him, had built his marker 20 feet short of the apex of a text-book example of an oil-bearing "dome".

In fact, geologist Ralph Rhoades had assessed Bahrain's potential some three years earlier, when in November 1927 he had been sent by Eastern Gulf Oil Company, an American corporation, to map the island. Rhoades found on Bahrain a perfect structure, a "dome" or fold, but without drilling he had no way of knowing its precise orientation, let alone whether there was oil in it.

So when oil flowed from a depth of 2008 ft (612 metres) on 1st June 1932, less than a year after Bahrain's first well had been "spudded in" (16th October 1931), it was a just tribute to Fred Davies' instinct. Although the flow was small and there was not much gas, the great thing was that oil had been found and Bahrain was to become the first oil-field to be developed in the Southern Arabian Gulf.

Fig. 2: Diagrammatic East-West Geological Section through the centre of Bahrain island illustrating the "fold" formation and oil-field "dome"

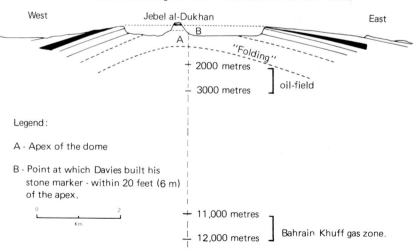

15

Plate 9:
"Spudding-In"
the first oil-we[ll]

16

However, this achievement produced little excitement locally, and so BAPCO started to drill another well. On Christmas Day 1932 an ecstatic Frank Holmes summoned Charles Belgrave, Shaikh Hamed's adviser, to come at once to the oil-field where well number 2 had "come in" with a rush. Belgrave recalled that it was a bitterly cold day and when he and his wife reached the well in the Jebel Dukhan foothills, they saw great ponds of black oil and black rivulets flowing down the wadis. "Oil, or what looked to us like smoke, but which was in fact gas, spouted gustily from the drilling rig and all the machinery and the men who were working were dripping with oil. It was not a pretty sight but it was an exciting moment for me. I could see, without any doubt that there was an oil-field in Bahrain. It was a great day for Major Holmes, who now saw visible proof of what he had always believed".

However, abbreviating history is always risky as events may appear over-simplified or dramatised - sometimes both. Perhaps, in order to do justice to the highly complex operation of oil-field exploration and to the people associated with it, it is relevant to pause for a moment and consider the circumstances of Bahrain's oil heritage. Why does Bahrain have oil? For that matter, what is it?

Petroleum, it would seem, forms through the decomposition of various types of marine life - chiefly plankton, but also algae and lowly animal organisms. As the remains of these organisms collect on the floors of seas and estuaries, they are gradually covered by deposits of thick fine sediment that exclude light and air, and prevent normal decay. Instead, partial decomposition transforms the original organic material into globules of petroleum. It is also thought that chemical reactions involving mineral salts contained in surrounding water and silt play a further part in the decomposition process.

As sedimentation continues, compression of the mass of the silt leads to its consolidation into rock measures of various kinds. The newly-formed globules, widely dispersed throughout the silt and intermingled with water-drops, are then squeezed from their parent rock, and forced to migrate. With them go the water and natural gas (also a product of organic decomposition) to any near-by rock seams such as limestone and sandstone, where the slow process of separation begins. Oil, being lighter, then floats to the top of the denser liquid, water. Gradually it collects in small pools, above which a quantity of natural gas forms.

So that the scattered oil globules can concentrate in one place, some slight disturbance or irregularity of the rock measures would seem to be necessary, for without such a "trap" or basin oilfields would not occur, at least not in a form conducive to commercial exploitation. It would seem that folding and dislocation in the rock measures provides such "traps", petroleum being associated with the outer margins of the folds. Finally, an impermeable rock layer is required to act as a seal immediately above the porous oil-bearing rock, without which petroleum would not concentrate in large quantities. This having been said, it is fairly obvious to conclude that the geological conditions in the Middle East are favourable to a remarkable extent for the occurrence of oil. The present strategic importance of its oil-fields in the world economy emphasises the point. However, Bahrain's oil resources were found at a time when there was no such certainty of commercial viability, but fortuitously at a time when the islands' major industry of pearling was going into decline. Although comparatively small by world standards, Bahrain's oil-field was to make a major contribution to the subsequent industrial growth of the nation.

GAS, as just explained, is an inevitable companion to oil in its natural state. Formerly there were two types of gas produced in Bahrain - Arab and Khuff gas. Arab gas is no longer produced, but Khuff (meaning camel's footprint) is peculiar to the Arabian Gulf. It is a zone of natural gas in reservoir form, its availability being dependent upon the depth of the reserve in varying parts of the field. As a result, there is no standard depth for drilling. The extent of Bahrain's natural gas-field is not certain, but estimates put the reserves at sufficient for a further forty years' supply. Extraction of this resource for industrial consumption is also accompanied by its injection back into the oil reserves in order to maintain equilibrium.

Associated gas, from which butane, propane and naptha may be removed in liquid compressed form, is a by-product of oil production, as is residue gas which has wide industrial applications.

GYPSUM, sometimes known as Djiss or Jus, has been used for building purposes in Bahrain for thousands of years, certainly since the Bronze Age tumuli builders lined their tombs with the prepared substance. In its natural state, gypsum lies just below the ground surface as an evaporite mineral, that is, in a sedimentary form as a result of the evaporation of saline water. Usually it is found in clays and limestone, the latter being readily evident in Bahrain in many places including, as mentioned already, the Howar Islands.

It is often prepared on the spot where it is quarried by interspersing it with layers of wood and slate, and then "firing" the pile. The slabs of quarried gypsum are then removed and beaten into a fine powder, which when mixed with water acts like a cement. Its quick-setting character lends itself as a powder base for mortar which may be used to bind stones in masonry work, or more particularly as a plaster coating. Craftsmen responsible for house ornamentation have used gypsum for their decorative carving which may be seen on many of the old houses in Bahrain.

3. HISTORY

LEGEND OF DILMUN

For many people the name of Bahrain is synonymous with Dilmun, whilst others like to think that it may have been the Garden of Eden. It is not the purpose of this guide to offer startling new material which adds to the debate, nor to come to any outstanding conclusions. Several learned scholars have made the Dilmun question part of their life's work, and even after years of earnest study no definitive answer has emerged. However enough convincing evidence exists for it to make fascinating and plausible reading, which at the very least gives a colourful background to a civilisation which flourished five thousand years ago.

The certainty is that from the 3rd millennium B.C., until the time of Cyrus of Persia, there is repeated mention in cuneiform texts of a land lying somewhere to the south of Babylonia called *Dilmun or Tilmun*. In the Sumerian language, the name is often written as *Ni-Tukki*, which some scholars interpret as "the place of the bringing of oil". This in itself is intriguing bearing in mind that the 20th century oilfields occur in what were the ancient Near-Eastern Empires. The name also occurs under the form of *Kur-Ni-Tuk* "the mountain of Dilmun" as well as being the place-name *Niduk-ki* which appears in the Babylonian myth of the Creation. But to appreciate even these conclusions, it is worth starting with nineteenth-century Mesopotamia.

Plate 10:
Map of the world

In 1839, an Englishman named Austen Henry Layard began excavating the Palace of Nineveh. There he found over twenty-five thousand cuneiform clay tablets, with wedge-shaped characters. During the 1888-9 seasons at Nippur, an American expedition led by John Punnet Peters, discovered between thirty and forty thousand similar tablets. As Henry Rawlinson began work on their decipherment in Baghdad where he was stationed, the task ahead of him was immense to say the least. It also became clear that the fragments contained poems, albeit incomplete in their narrative, representing some of the world's finest surviving literature, of high quality and unique character, antedating Homer's *Iliad*.

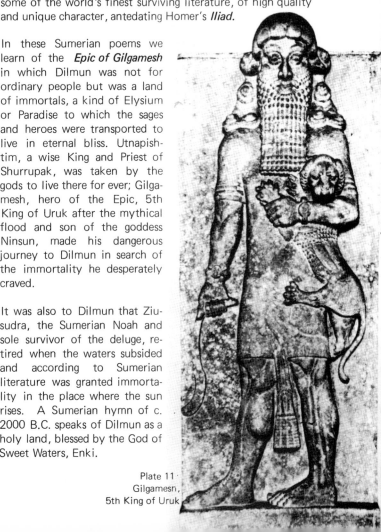

In these Sumerian poems we learn of the *Epic of Gilgamesh* in which Dilmun was not for ordinary people but was a land of immortals, a kind of Elysium or Paradise to which the sages and heroes were transported to live in eternal bliss. Utnapishtim, a wise King and Priest of Shurrupak, was taken by the gods to live there for ever; Gilgamesh, hero of the Epic, 5th King of Uruk after the mythical flood and son of the goddess Ninsun, made his dangerous journey to Dilmun in search of the immortality he desperately craved.

It was also to Dilmun that Ziusudra, the Sumerian Noah and sole survivor of the deluge, retired when the waters subsided and according to Sumerian literature was granted immortality in the place where the sun rises. A Sumerian hymn of c. 2000 B.C. speaks of Dilmun as a holy land, blessed by the God of Sweet Waters, Enki.

Plate 11
Gilgamesh,
5th King of Uruk

There is also a very old account of Dilmun, written on a tablet from Nippur, which describes how, when the world was young and the work of creation had only just begun, Dilmun was the place where "the croak of the raven was not heard, the bird of death did not utter a cry of death, the lion did not devour, the wolf did not rend the lamb, the dove did not mourn, there was no widow, no sickness, no old age, no lamentation".

Moving from the Sumerian tales of immortality to the Assyrian texts, we learn more of the earthly practice of sea-faring. About 2,300 B.C. Sargon the Great, the Semitic Ruler who conquered and controlled much of the ancient near-eastern world (at least for a short time), recorded on the memorial steles and statues which he erected at Nippur that boats of Dilmun tied up in his newly-built capital, Agade. Towards the end of the eighth century (710) B.C., Sargon II of Assyria recorded that he had received presents from Uperi, King of Dilmun, "who lives like a fish 30 double hours away in the midst of the sea of the rising sun", a double hour, or beru, being equal to 10.7 kilometres.

Sir Henry Rawlinson, who deciphered cuneiform more than a century ago, was the first scholar to suggest that Bahrain might have been the site of Dilmun. He based his theory on the discovery of a cuneiform inscription on a basalt block, found by Captain Durand in 1879 built into one of the mosques in Bahrain's Al-Khamis district. Dating back to 2,000 B.C. it names the God Inzak as the Head of the Agarum Tribe.

Since then several scholars have discussed the possible location of Dilmun. Professor Cornwall favours all of the Bahrain area and a part of the Eastern coast of Saudi Arabia and Kuwait. Professor Kramer suggests that new inscriptional material which has become available in recent years indicates that, whatever its western boundary, Dilmun extended much further to the east and included much, if not all, of that part of Iran, Pakistan and India, on which flourished the Indus or Harappan civilisation.

It now seems clear that the island "with abundant fresh water, lying some two days' sail with a following wind from Mesopotamia", was Bahrain, and the centre of urban life for at least 3,000 years before the Christian era. In the centuries around 2,000 B.C. it was clearly a place of considerable wealth and power, with close cultural and trading contacts with the Sumerians of Mesopotamia and the Indus Valley. The most recent reference to Dilmun so far discovered dates from 544 B.C., after which the name seems to have been forgotten.

As Geoffrey Bibby commented more than a decade ago, "the Dilmun problem is not whether Bahrain was part of Dilmun - the big problem is why was Dilmun so important to the people of South Mesopotamia? Why were the sites of the earliest myths of gods and heroes in a land which for 2,000 years was an independent kingdom across the sea? Why did it denote a land of immortality, a holy land? It is to those questions that archaeology can not, as yet, give an answer."

However, as the author of the English translation of the *Epic of Gilgamesh* explains, further evidence may yet be found to solve these problems. When the many thousands of tablet pieces were removed from Nineveh to the British Museum (London) and from Nippur to museums in Philadelphia (USA) and Istanbul (Turkey), scholars were faced with the mammoth task of cross-referencing their sources across the world. Added to this, the division of the material complicated the work of decipherment for in some cases one half of an important tablet would be stored in America whilst the other half would be located in Istanbul. Before the contents of the tablet could be understood, both halves, or copies of them, had to be brought together.

It may be that as the work on these tablets continues more than a century after their discovery, the missing pieces of the Sumerian poems may be identified, and if scholars are lucky they may learn more about the intriguing civilisation of Dilmun.

PRE-HISTORY

Approximately one hundred thousands years ago, Europe and North America are thought to have been in the last phases of

the Ice Age while Bahrain was enjoying an equable and tempe-
rate climate, perhaps comparable with that of Greece today.
At that time, the world sea level was one hundred metres
below its present level.

The results of a recent excavation conducted at Al-Markh,[1]
a fish midden[2] south of Zellaq[3], imply that as Europe entered
the final stages of the Ice-Age the Arabian Gulf may have been
dry, or watered only by the Tigris and Euphrates and other
rivers flowing down from the Zagros Mountains.

Thousands of flints evident on the desert flats and rocky
slopes of the main island lie most thickly on a line running
south from the Awali-Zellaq Road (Highway 105) about 3
kilometres inland. They are scattered in abundance elsewhere,
their distribution density depending upon whether or not the
original ground surface has been covered subsequently with
sand drift, cultivation or settlements. These early flints do
not tell us a great deal about the life-style of the hunters who
inhabited the islands approximately ten thousand years ago.
However, the subsequent introduction of agriculture gave
rise to a new range of flint implements within two thousand
years, indicating a transition from a Stone Age livelihood
based on hunting to the early practice of land utilisation and
harvesting.

It is now believed that Bahrain was connected to mainland
Arabia until 6,000 B.C. and it seems likely that any settlement in the Gulf before Bahrain was an island would have
been either on the sea shore or along one of the rivers and so
would subsequently have been drowned by the rise in sea-
level. This is demonstrated at Al-Markh, which by 3,800 B.C.
was located on a small island lying off the west coast of what
had become the main island of Bahrain. "Ubaid" pottery
found at this site is among the earliest to be excavated in
Bahrain and suggests trading contact with the Mesopotamian
settlement of that name, located on the Euphrates river.

---

1 - Roaf, M. - Seminar for Arabian Studies, Vol. 6. 1976 - p. 159
2 - Fish Midden - deposit of discarded fish bones
3 - Zellaq - modern settlement on the west coast of Bahrain island

Less than a thousand years later (c. 3,000 B.C.) the State of Dilmun is thought to have been established with its commercial centre in Bahrain. An outstanding monument of over one hundred thousand burial mounds, attributed to this and subsequent phases of Bahrain's history, comprises what is believed to be the largest pre-historic cemetery in the world.

About 2000 B.C. Dilmun's importance began to decline. At the same time, (according to recent radiocarbon dates), Indo-European tribes called Aryans invaded present-day Pakistan and destroyed the cities of the Indus valley civilisation. The impact on Bahrain was immediate. Trade goods from India were cut off and the islands had to fall back on their own resources.

Plate 12: A few of Bahrain's burial mounds

With the rise of the Assyrian Empire, whose capital was Nineveh on the upper Tigris in Mesopotamia, and its conquest of Babylonia prior to 900 B.C., a degree of prosperity appears to have returned to Bahrain. From 750 B.C. onwards the Assyrian kings repeatedly claimed sovereignty over the islands, although it would appear that this overlordship was contingent entirely upon the naval strength of the Mesopotamian rulers. About this time the Aryan princes had picked up the pieces of their own disrupted civilisation, and trading contact was re-established between India and the Arabian Gulf.

However the renewed wealth of Bahrain did not escape the attention of the Babylonian kingdom to the north and shortly after 600 B.C. Dilmun was incorporated into their new empire. A Babylonian was appointed as the Provincial Governor, that is until the Persians conquered the islands c. 540 B.C., having already sacked Nineveh in the 7th century B.C.

After the fall of the Mesopotamian civilisations, no foreign power seems to have controlled eastern Arabia until early in the fourth century B.C. This probably accounts for Dilmun disappearing from mention in cuneiform texts about this time. It is now that we move to the period of Bahrain's history which is contemporary with Classical Greece, and Alexander the Great's ambitions.

CLASSICAL YEARS

After the fall of the Assyrian Empire we hear no more of Bahrain until Alexander the Great embarked on his Macedonian adventure. At the age of twenty-two he had aspirations to unify the Middle East into one lasting Empire and set about this aim by despatching his senior officers to the Punjab and Sind. When they returned victorious, Alexander planned his next campaign by sending three vessels on voyages of exploration down the Arabian Gulf. Two of these ships sailed only as far as Tylos, which has been identified beyond doubt as the islands of Bahrain. Pliny not only describes their position exactly, but adds that Tylos was extremely famous for its numerous pearls. There the Greeks found Bahrain ruled once more by an independent King and evidence suggests that trade with Greece prospered at this time.

However, Alexander's untimely death in June 323 B.C. at the age of 32 years and 10 months, left only his chief generals to battle for the empire he visualised. After over 20 years of upheaval and struggle, a pattern began to emerge. Ptolemy took Egypt, Antipater and Cassander shared Macedonia and Greece, Antigonous briefly controlled Western Asia, whilst Seleucus and his family took Syria, Babylon and the rest of Asia which embraced Bahrain. It is to this period of the Seleucid Dynasty that many of the grave-mounds located on either side of Bahrain's Budaiya Highway are ascribed. They are contemporary with the artistic zenith of the Greek Hellenistic Age, prior to Rome becoming the arbiter of Middle East affairs when Constantine moved his capital east to modern Istanbul, to control his eastern provinces.

Throughout Bahrain's Seleucid Period 300-0 B.C. and the Parthian Period 0-300 A.D., the islands enjoyed commercial prosperity. For the last few centuries before the coming of Islam, it would appear that Bahrain was dominated by Arab tribes from the mainland, at least until the fourth century A.D., when Shappur II, the Sassanian King of Persia, annexed the country.

THE COMING OF ISLAM

We now enter a particularly significant period in Bahrain's history, for it is in the 7th century A.D. that the Moslem conquests of the Middle East occurred, followed by widespread adherence to Islam. When the faith was introduced to Bahrain, the nation was governed for Persia by a Christian Arab. Apparently during this period there were a number of Nestorian dioceses in the Gulf area, one of which was situated in Bahrain. It appears, however, that Christianity was not the dominant religion in Bahrain at the period of its conversion to Islam, although chroniclers do not specify the nature of the local faith.

It is from this time that the Hijriya calendar based on the moon's thirty-day phases was adopted by the Islamic world. When speaking of Bahrain's history from this point, it would be more appropriate and technically correct for us to change our dating method too. However, in order to avoid confusion to those readers unfamiliar with the Hijriya calendar, we shall continue from where we were speaking of the 7th century in the previous paragraph (according to the Gregorian calendar), rather than complicate our chronology by moving ahead from now on with the Islamic year, 1 A.H.

MEDIAEVAL CENTURIES

For the next 350 years (up to the 11th Century) Bahrain and Eastern Arabia were ruled by governors on behalf of the Caliphs of Damascus and Baghdad, but from time to time there were politico-religious revolts against the central authority. As a result, both Shia and Kharajite schismatics sought rufuge on the Bahrain islands. An offspring of the extreme Ismaili sect, but with many other contributing features, was the Carmathian movement, whose first ruler in Eastern Arabia was Abu Sa'id al-Jannabi. It was during his reign, in 903, that the Carmathians seized Hajar and many of the inhabitants fled to the islands of Bahrain.

About the year 1058, Abu-l-Bahlul, one of Bahrain's leading inhabitants, revolted against Carmathian rule and proclaimed himself Prince. Promptly he defeated a Carmathian army sent against him and appealed to the Caliph in Baghdad for aid and recognition, but his victory was short-lived for he was soon to be driven from Bahrain by the Ruler of Qatif, Yahya bin Abbas. The turbulence continued unabated, for war soon followed between Yahya's successors and Abdulla al-Ayuni, who had succeeded the Carmathians in Hasa. Finally Ayuni triumphed and together with his family seized Bahrain to rule the islands for many years. Although little is known about this period, two surviving monuments in Bahrain are the Mosque Suq-Al-Khamis on the modern Sh. Sulman Highway, whose first phase is ascribed to this period, and the Islamic Fort attributed to the Carmathian settlement (see Routes 5 and 8).

We now move forward a century to 1154 when the famous Arab-Spanish geographer, Idrisi, gave a remarkably accurate description of Bahrain, telling us amongst other things that "the island is governed by an independent chief. The inhabitants of the two banks are satisfied with his justice and his piety".

There are several extant descriptions of Bahrain in the 14th century, a period in which it would appear the islands changed hands many times. Early in the 15th century, Bahrain was united with Qatif and Hasa under Shaikh Ibrahim al-Maliki and in 1487 a tyrannical reign was ended by an Omani invasion and the appointment of 'Umar bin al-Khattab as governor.

THE PORTUGUESE CAMPAIGN

After Vasco da Gama the great Portuguese explorer had reached India between 1497 and 1499, his followers began to establish strategic locations throughout the Far East, the Indian Ocean and the Arabian Gulf, for the purpose of taking over the spice trade that had been handled for so long and so remuneratively by Arab traders. The Arabian Gulf was to become the westernmost and northernmost outpost within the entire 16th century eastern empire of the Portuguese maritime state. On capturing Goa on the west coast of India in 1510, the Portuguese were quick to realise that, in order to secure this position, they would have to gain control over Hormuz at the mouth of the Arabian Gulf and Aden at the mouth of the Red Sea, whereupon Alfonso de Alburquerque captured Hormuz and set about developing it into a trading centre.

A chain-reaction had begun, for the Ruler of Hormuz in 1515 was a vassal of the Shah of Persia; the Ruler of Bahrain was under the suzerainty of Hormuz. As soon as the Portuguese moved in they demanded tribute from Hormuz, which in turn demanded homage from Bahrain. Predictably, Bahrain did not react kindly to this, revolted against the new Suzerain of Hormuz, only to be occupied immediately by Portuguese auxiliaries from India and the lower Gulf. Thus in 1521 the islands of Bahrain fell into Portuguese hands, following which the Bahrain Fort was built (see Route 8). The year 1529 saw another challenge to Portuguese authority in Bahrain, brought about by their exiling of the Wezir of Hormuz, a relative of the Governor of Bahrain, for refusing to pay additional taxes. The Bahraini Governor copied his relative's example, so causing the Portuguese to despatch a fleet north to attack the fort. As their gunpowder ran out, so did their luck. The expedition, reduced by fever to a token force, was given aid by the Governor who feared reprisals if he destroyed the last vestiges of the Portuguese presence. However, when the ailing crew set sail again, bad weather compounded their ill-fortune, and the remains of the fleet were sunk by a storm.

Plate 14: N.W. Bastion of the Portuguese Fort

By 1535 a great power dominated each end of the Arabian Gulf: the Turks at the northern end and the Portuguese in the south, with Bahrain in between. The two opponents moved steadily against each other as they fought for control of the spice trade in the Indian Ocean. The Arab chieftains of Basra (southern Iraq) did not like Turkish control and so sought the aid of the Portuguese. At the southern end of the Arabian Gulf the Ruler of Hormuz, who disliked Portuguese rule, sought the aid of the Turks. Bahrain stood vulnerably in the middle, but by some fortune and diplomacy the Bahrain islands managed to maintain a middle-man position.

1560 marked the end of the long conflict between Turkey and the Portuguese Empire over control of the Arabian Gulf but Bahrain remained in vassalage to Hormuz and the Portuguese until 1602.

It appears from Portuguese records that during the last forty years of the sixteenth century Bahrain managed to retain its strategic buffer position. It also seems that neither local wars, piracy nor international struggles interfered very seriously with the prosperity and the relative peace which the islands were now enjoying.

The immediate cause for the expulsion of the Portuguese from Bahrain was the behaviour of their governor, a relative, as we have learned, of the King of Hormuz. He set the seal on a most tyrannical rule by the murder, in 1602, of a wealthy and respected Bahraini in order to gain control over his wealth, especially his famous pearl collection. The victim's brother, Rukn ed-Din, having first gained the confidence of the murderer, slew him and with the aid of the people seized the fort. He then put himself under the protection of the Persians, Portugal's main rivals in the Arabian Gulf, who withstood a counter-attack and then took over the islands.

For many years the Portuguese would not accept defeat. Eventually, in 1645 a fleet set out from India to destroy Hormuz and Bahrain, but the mission was destined to failure. Omani pirates destroyed it before it had even entered the Arabian Gulf. Until the end of the sixteenth century a series of Persian governors ruled Bahrain with the aid of a garrison of some 300 men, but at the turn of the century the Omanis invaded Bahrain. A period of havoc and suffering ensued, with the Persians purchasing Bahrain from the Omanis in 1720 for a large sum of money.

THE AL-KHALIFA LINE OF SUCCESSION

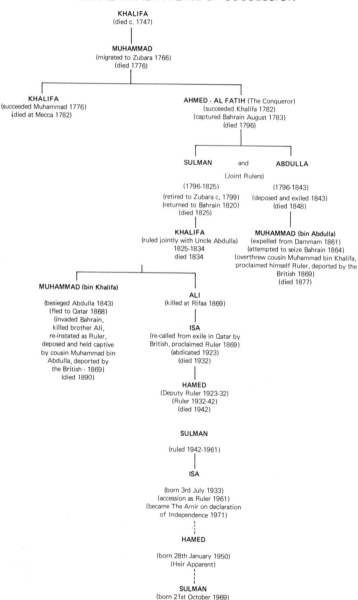

KHALIFA
(died c. 1747)

MUHAMMAD
(migrated to Zubara 1766)
(died 1776)

KHALIFA
(succeeded Muhammad 1776)
(died at Mecca 1782)

AHMED - AL FATIH (The Conqueror)
(succeeded Khalifa 1782)
(captured Bahrain August 1783)
(died 1796)

SULMAN and **ABDULLA**

(Joint Rulers)

(1796-1825)
(retired to Zubara c. 1799)
(returned to Bahrain 1820)
(died 1825)

(1796-1843)
(deposed and exiled 1843)
(died 1848)

KHALIFA
(ruled jointly with Uncle Abdulla)
1825-1834
died 1834

MUHAMMAD (bin Abdulla)
(expelled from Dammam 1861)
(attempted to seize Bahrain 1864)
(overthrew cousin Muhammad bin Khalifa,
proclaimed himself Ruler, deported by the
British 1869)
(died 1877)

MUHAMMAD (bin Khalifa)

(besieged Abdulla 1843)
(fled to Qatar 1868)
(invaded Bahrain,
killed brother Ali,
re-instated as Ruler,
deposed and held captive
by cousin Muhammad bin
Abdulla, deported by
the British - 1869)
(died 1890)

ALI
(killed at Rifaa 1869)

ISA
(re-called from exile in Qatar by
British, proclaimed Ruler 1869)
(abdicated 1923)
(died 1932)

HAMED
(Deputy Ruler 1923-32)
(Ruler 1932-42)
(died 1942)

SULMAN

(ruled 1942-1961)

ISA

(born 3rd July 1933)
(accession as Ruler 1961)
(became The Amir on declaration
of Independence 1971)

HAMED

(born 28th January 1950)
(Heir Apparent)

SULMAN
(born 21st October 1969)

32

THE AL-KHALIFA DYNASTY

The Al-Khalifa family can trace its origin back to early 18th century Kuwait, when it was founded by a Khalifa of the tribe formerly known as Utub. When Khalifa died c. 1747, his son Muhammad migrated to Zubara on the west coast of Qatar in order to be nearer the Bahrain pearling industry. It was not long afterwards that he was joined by other members of the family, who consolidated their position at Zubara by building a large town and a great fort, Qala'at Marir, the ruins of which still stand today.

It was from Qatar that the Al-Khalifa family paid friendly pearl-buying visits to Bahrain and established a presence on the islands. Meanwhile Muhammad died in 1776, to be succeeded by his son Khalifa. However, Khalifa bin Muhammad's term as head of the family was abbreviated somewhat unexpectedly when he died in 1782, whilst on pilgrimage to Mecca.

By 1783 local sensitivities both in Bahrain and Qatar were delicate, exacerbated by the Persians' attack on Zubara and their engagement of the Al-Khalifas in combat. The Sabah of Kuwait, seeing his cousins under siege, despatched a fleet to Bahrain to assist the Al-Khalifa family led by Ahmed, Khalifa bin Muhammad's brother, who, on triumphing in Qatar, attacked Bahrain to drive out the Persian garrison controlling the islands.

It was as a result of the Al-Khalifa victory that Shaikh Ahmed al-Fatih (The Conqueror) occupied Bahrain and set about developing an impressive mercantile fleet with an equally powerful pearl trade portfolio. When he died in 1796, he was succeeded jointly by his sons Abdulla and Sulman, although it was the latter who was more occupied with the affairs of Bahrain than his brother, for Abdulla eventually founded the Al-Abdulla branch of the family while living in exile in Saudi Arabia.

Three years later, in 1799, the Imam of Muscat sent a fleet to occupy Bahrain. The Omanis, on gaining a footing, built the Arad fort on Muharraq island's south shore, the site of a former Portuguese military installation. It was also at this time that the Wahabi tribe occupied the islands for a short time, and Shaikh Sulman bin Ahmed Al-Khalifa, considering himself unable to repel the invaders, retired to Zubara. After the height of the pirate period, Sulman returned to Bahrain, and in February 1820 the joint rulers of Bahrain, Shaikhs Sulman and Abdulla, signed the "General Treaty" between the East India Company and Bahrain.

When Shaikh Sulman died in 1825, he was succeeded by his son Khalifa bin Sulman who shared power with his uncle, the aged Shaikh Abdulla. However, in 1834 nephew Khalifa died, leaving Abdulla as sole ruler who, unable to control the ambitions of the younger members of the family, found his authority being challenged by his great-nephew, Muhammed bin Khalifa bin Sulman Al-Khalifa.

After a period during which Muhammad held Muharraq island, and Abdulla held Manama town on Bahrain island, Muhammad was forced to take refuge on the Arabian mainland, where he sought new allies. He subsequently seized the fort at Zubara and in the spring of 1843 landed on Bahrain. He quickly captured Manama and besieged his great-uncle Abdulla at Abu Mahur fort on Muharraq island.

Finally, Shaikh Abdulla gave in and was permitted to live in exile with his family on the mainland, while Muhammad his great-nephew continued to enjoy a relatively trouble-free reign. In 1861 he signed a Treaty of Perpetual Peace and Friendship with the British concerning matters of slavery, maritime aggression and trade; but, this notwithstanding, the peace of the islands was upset by intermittent raids by his cousin, also named Muhammad, son of the Abdulla who had since died in exile in Bushire. However, in the same year as the signing of the Treaty, the British expelled Muhammad bin Abdulla from Dammam although he remained in the Arabian Gulf for some time.

After six years years of peace, war broke out between the Qataris and the Al-Khalifa family. The result was that Muhammad bin Khalifa fled to Qatar; the fort of Abu Mahur near Muharraq town was destroyed and the Bahraini fleet was scuttled. Upon Muhammad's flight, his brother Ali bin Khalifa succeeded as Ruler of Bahrain. The outcome was that the

British forced the new Ruler, Shaikh Ali, to pay a fine of 100,000 Maria Theresa dollars for breach of the Treaty, while his brother Muhammad was forbidden to return to Bahrain. However, even this episode did not deter the persistent Muhammad bin Khalifa, for within a year he had built up a force with which he invaded Bahrain in September 1869, attacked Rifaa Fort, killed his brother Ali and promptly declared himself Ruler once more. The irony of this episode was that, having appointed his exiled cousin Muhammad bin Abdulla as a lieutenant in his army, Muhammad bin Khalifa was over-thrown by his disloyal relation and imprisoned by him later that year, thus enabling Muhammad bin Abdulla to proclaim himself Ruler.

Plate 15: Shaikh Isa the First

This turbulent state of affairs was anything but in the spirit of the Treaty of Perpetual Peace and Friendship which the now captive ex-Ruler had signed some years earlier. As a result, the British despatched the Consul from Bushire in a man-of-war to try and restore some stability to the islands. The newly-proclaimed Shaikh Muhammad bin Abdulla, and his imprisoned rival cousin Muhammad bin Khalifa, were deported to Bombay, while Isa, son of Ali killed at Rifaa, was summoned from exile in Qatar to be acclaimed Ruler of Bahrain at the age of 21. At last Bahrain was to enjoy a period of calm and stability, although even Shaikh Isa the First's apparently unquestioned reign of 54 years had its problems.

The Turks and the Persians laid claim to the islands; at the same time Bahrain was threatened constantly with attacks by the Arab tribes of Qatar. However, the presence of British men-of-war in the Gulf deterred any active attempt at invasion, whilst Shaikh Isa undertook not to import and export arms, nor to allow any foreign power to intervene in the government of Bahrain. Notwithstanding this caution, Shaikh Isa was to take no chances. In order to avoid a recurrence of the dynastic disputes which had beset the islands for so long, Shaikh Isa took the prudent step in 1898 of appointing his eldest son Shaikh Hamed as Heir Apparent.

20TH CENTURY

In 1902 a British Political Agent was posted to Bahrain and in 1913 a Convention was signed which included the recognition of Bahrain's independence and of her control of a number of islands near her, including the Howar Group, which although closer to the Qatari coast remain today under the jurisdiction of the State of Bahrain. During 1923 seventy-five year-old Shaikh Isa retired from active participation in the affairs of State, whereupon the Heir Apparent assumed the role of Deputy Ruler for the next nine years.

When Shaikh Isa died on 9th December 1932, he had witnessed the dawn of a new economic era in Bahrain's history, for just six months earlier oil had been struck at Well Number One near the Jebel Dukhan. In the same year, Bahrain's telephone service was inaugurated and the first Imperial Airways machine landed at Bahrain on its way to India.

Plate 16: Shaikh Hamed bin Isa Al-Khalifa with two of his sons (foreground). Major Frank Holmes is wearing the tropical helmet.

During Shaikh Hamed's reign the centuries' old pearl industry slipped into final decline. However, the rapid growth of oil exploration compensated for its demise, enabling work to commence on BAPCO's oil refinery by 1935. During the following year the first link in what was to become Bahrain's impressive Causeway network was opened to road traffic, although the toll-gate connecting Shaikh Hamed Causeway to Muharraq and Manama towns did not become fully operational until 1942. The six-year delay was the result of enemy action during World War II destroying two shipments of steel for the construction of the swing-bridge whilst en route from Europe.

Plate 17: Shaikh Sulman bin Hamed Al-Khalifa visiting the oil refinery (late 1950s)

It was also in 1942 that Shaikh Hamed died at his country palace at Sakhir. Shaikh Sulman, his son and the present Amir's father, succeeded him in February of that year and was to rule for almost 20 years. The first half of the 1950s saw considerable progress in the public and social services, particularly health and education. 1953 was marked by the Government ceasing to calculate budgets and salaries according to the Hijriya Calendar. Since this time the Gregorian Calendar has been used for official accounting purposes. In August 1955 the Bahrain Broadcasting Station (BBS) came on air.

The second half of the decade was a time of political and administrative advance, noted by the establishment of a system of Councils enabling the population to participate more actively in the affairs of the country. In the field of international relations, a significant event in Shaikh Sulman's reign was his visit to Saudi Arabia in 1958 for a meeting with the Saudi monarch, King Saud. As a result, an agreement was signed between the two rulers providing for the sharing of the profits derived from any oil found in an area of sea that had hitherto been the subject of dispute between the two countries.

SHAIKH ISA BIN SULMAN AL-KHALIFA'S REIGN

On 16th December 1961 Shaikh Isa's Accession Ceremony was celebrated, his father Shaikh Sulman having passed away a month previously in the peaceful surroundings of a country house near West Rifaa. The present Amir is the tenth member of the Al-Khalifa family to rule Bahrain since the islands were conquered by his ancestor in 1782.

Highlights of the early years of Shaikh Isa's reign were the establishment of the Bahrain Currency Board in 1964, the issue of the first national currency, the dinar[1], in October 1965 and in 1967 the opening of Mina Sulman, Bahrain's deep water port named after the late Ruler.

Perhaps the most impressive achievement of the 1960s was the

1 - The previous currency was the Indian External Rupee.
   In 1965 one Bahraini dinar = 10 Indian Rupees.

inauguration in 1968 of the Amir's personal brainchild, Isa Town, a project which owed its inception to Shaikh Isa's generosity by donating the land for the site. The State has provided the town's services and public buildings free of charge, whilst only the actual cost of the houses has been borne by the residents who, by stipulation, are Bahraini citizens. It was also in 1968 that the National Guard, later to become the Bahrain Defence Force (BDF) was formed under the command of H.E. Shaikh Hamed bin Isa Al-Khalifa, the present Crown Prince. In the last year of the decade (1969) Bahrain's Earth Station at Ras Abu Jarjur on the main island's east coast was opened. Preparation for the islands' independence was marked in 1970 by the formation of the Council of State, whose duties were taken over when the first Cabinet was formed in 1971, following Shaikh Isa's Declaration of Bahrain as an independent Sovereign State on 14th August of that year. The following day a New Treaty of Friendship was signed between Bahrain and Great Britain.

Alongside Bahrain's formalised system of administration is the traditional system of public accessibility which has been followed for many years. Shaikh Isa, like his father and grandfather, sits in open majlis (reception) for many hours weekly at his Palace in West Rifaa. It is during these sessions that any Bahraini is able to have direct access to the Amir.

1971 was noted for Bahrain's admission as a member of the United Nations and the International Monetary Fund. In 1973 the State of Bahrain joined OAPEC, the Organisation of Arab Petroleum Exporting Countries.

By the middle of the 1970s, Bahrain had consolidated its position as an international commercial centre and developing industrial nation. This was manifested by the formation in November 1974 of the Bahrain Monetary Agency as the Central Bank, superseding the Currency Board. Work also began on Bahrain's prestigious dry dock which was to be financed by OAPEC.

Three years later in 1977 two more links in Bahrain's Causeway network were completed. The Arab Shipbuilding and Repair Yard officially opened its $340 million dry-dock complex, which is located on 300,000 square metres of reclaimed land reached by a 7-kilometre new causeway south of Hidd town on Muharraq island. The other causeway, between Bahrain and Sitra islands, forms a strategic link between BAPCO's storage "tank farm" and refinery, the aluminium industry's smelter and extrusion plants, and the free transit cargo port and container terminal at Mina Sulman.

Moving ahead to the present, 1981 marks the tenth anniversary of Bahrain's independence, and the 20th anniversary of Shaikh Isa bin Sulman Al-Khalifa's accession as the Ruler of Bahrain. Quite apart from other anniversaries of note, such as the golden jubilee of the "spudding-in" of the first oil well, and the silver jubilee of Bahrain's National Bank, it has been a significant year in its own right.

On the 27th April the results of the National Census conducted earlier that month were announced, revealing that the present population of Bahrain is 358,857, an increase of 142,779 since the last census was taken in 1971.

At the end of April, the much-discussed plan to establish the Arabian Gulf University in Bahrain was given the go-ahead at a meeting held in Baghdad of the education ministers of the seven Gulf State sponsors: Bahrain, Iraq, Kuwait, Oman, Qatar, Saudi Arabia and the United Arab Emirates. The University is to be constructed under the auspices of the Arab Bureau of Education for the Gulf States on a site adjacent to the Awali-Zellaq Highway and Sakhir Palace, and is intended to accommodate 10,000 students by the year 2000 A.D.

In the early summer of 1981, Shaikh Isa bin Sulman Al-Khalifa attended what transpired to be a momentous occasion in the history of the Arabian peninsula. Hosted by the Emirate of Abu Dhabi, the first summit meeting of the newly-formed Gulf Co-operation Council (GCC) was held on 25th May. Attended by the Rulers of the States of Bahrain, Kuwait, Qatar, the Federation of the United Arab Emirates, the Kingdom of Saudi Arabia and the Sultanate of Oman, this powerful gathering pledged its commitment to Islamic solidarity, military autonomy and economic collaboration, including a proposed unified Gulf currency.

Two months later, on 8th July, after many years of negotiation and speculation, the contract for the construction of the $564 million Bahrain-Saudi Arabia Causeway was signed. The Dutch-led consortium that was awarded the contract anticipates that the 25-kilometre box-girder bridge and 4-lane highway will be operational in 225 weeks, thus linking the State of Bahrain to the mainland Kingdom of Saudi Arabia, and completing Bahrain's most impressive link yet in its Causeway network.

However, at the conclusion of this project, there will have been sacrifices also, for in the path of the motorway lie almost 600 burial mounds which will be destroyed in the course of its construction. An accelerated programme of excavation is being undertaken at present in order to rescue as much as possible before the demolition deadline.

Therefore perhaps it is appropriate that 1981 is also marked by the formation by Amiri Decree on 20th July of a new Directorate of Heritage, which together with the existing Directorate of Archaeology and Museums and new Directorate of Tourism, will ensure that the interests of Bahrain's antiquity are well served.

Plate 18:
Date Harvesting

4. TRADE

FROM PREHISTORY TO THE PRESENT

For many centuries, the Arabian Gulf has been one of the most important trade routes in the world. Topography and marine conditions have pre-determined this to a great extent, the islands of Bahrain especially offering sheltered anchorages and abundant supplies of fresh water for the ships plying between its northern and southern ports.

The existence of trade can be traced back to the third millennium B.C. when the City States of Mesopotamia traded with countries to their south and east. Three names are mentioned repeatedly in early cuneiform records, those of Dilmun, Magan and Meluhha. The Dilmun culture has as its two main strongholds Failaka (Island of Rock)[1], adjacent to Kuwait, and Bahrain, each of which is thought to have had some political and economic domination over certain parts of the adjacent Arabian mainland. Magan can almost certainly be identified as a country located on both sides of the entrance to the Arabian Gulf, present-day Oman and Baluchistan. The seafaring nation of Meluhha was apparently situated further east from Mesopotamia and has almost certainly been identified with the region of the Indus river, bordering on an Arabian Gulf sea-board.

It is known that both Magan and Meluhha were important to Dilmun, since as producers of copper, precious stones and several kinds of timber, including the durable sissoo wood used in boat-building, they provided the Dilmun civilisation with commodities which it lacked as natural resources.

After the Ur III period, in the early centuries of the 2nd millennium B.C., Bahrain appears to have been firmly established as a trans-shipment centre and main entrepot for Arabian Gulf supplies. Since the Seleucid and Parthian periods and time of Alexander the Great's expeditions, the Bahrain islands have been celebrated for their pearl fisheries. Not only did they have trading connections with the far east, but a flourishing market with the west was developing.

1 - Called Ecarus in the days of Alexandar the Great.

Plate 19: 3rd millennium B.C. trading ship

As early as the fourth century A.D. ships from what was then known as Persia had established direct trade links with China, a route which was to last until the tenth century when the great Tang dynasty fell. Evidence of Chinese porcelain excavated from contemporary occupation levels in Bahrain corroborates this theory as well as re-stating the islands' importance as a commercial centre.

In the tenth century A.D. three Arabian Gulf ports of importance were Basra (in the north, now present-day Iraq), Oman (in the south) and Siraf (the richest town in Persia). By the 11th century, the key position for Gulf trade was held by Hormuz, the island astride the narrow straits of the same name separating Arabian Gulf waters from the Gulf of Oman.

As we have already learned, by the 16th century the Portuguese had aspirations to conquer the spice trade in the area. They also cast a covetous eye on the pearl trade, but they were by no means the only people to do so. Pearl diving is the oldest industry in Bahrain and has been the reason why an otherwise small and comparatively unresourceful group of islands has been the scene of so many bitter wars and invading armies. It was not until the second half of the nineteenth century, partly as a result of the British fleet's policing of the islands' territorial waters and the Arabian Gulf's oyster beds, that the pearl divers and merchants could work and trade in relative peace.

By the turn of the nineteenth century the pearl industry had reached its peak, with Bahrain's share of the market then being calculated as £303,941.[1] However, as a luxury trade, it was hit very badly by the European financial depression in the 1920s, especially as Paris was a centre from which merchants visited Bahrain to negotiate their wares. By 1932, it was in an even more precarious state, suffering from competition from cultured pearls.

The 1945 season, as Sir Charles Belgrave recalls, was "the last flicker of prosperity from pearls; in the years that followed every season fewer boats went out to the pearl banks and more men gave up diving as they were attracted by steady, better-paid employment on shore".

It can be argued that it was either fate or coincidence that at the time of the pearl industry's decline a powerful catalyst in the form of oil exploration was to provide the impetus for the islands of Bahrain to develop an economy based on technology. The present Bahrain Government, aware of the dangers of dependence upon a single industry, is anxious to encourage a programme of diversification, thus avoiding an economic decline similar to that of 50 years ago when the oil reserves eventually begin to run dry.

Extensive industrialisation has already taken place, especially in the aluminium and ship-building industries. The traditional livelihoods of agriculture and fishing are being given Government support for research and training, as well as financial aid for the development of experimental farms and the building of six new fishing ports. The telecommunications industry which has developed rapidly in the last decade has facilitated Bahrain's emergence as the Middle East's leading banking centre, a "free-transit" maritime entrepot, and, it is hoped, a leading international bullion market.

1 - According to American Missionary, Zwemer, in 1896.

PEARLING

Arabian Gulf pearls are reputed to be the finest in the world and have been famous since ancient times. One of the earliest references to them is in a cuneiform inscription found in Nineveh (Iraq), which reads "in the sea of changeable winds (the Arabian Gulf) his merchants fished for pearls". Tylos, the classical name for Bahrain, was stated by Pliny to be "famous for the vast number of its pearls". The Holy Koran considered them property of paradise, a part of the combination composed of fairies, golden bracelets, and silk cloths[1] , while Abu Zaid Hassan described diving methods in the 10th century, demonstrating that there has been little change during the last thousand years.

Many later travellers and geographers have written accounts of the pearl fisheries, in particular Duarte Barbosa, a Portuguese explorer, who said of Barem (Bahrain) in 1485 "around it grows much seed pearl, also large pearls of good quality. The merchants of the island itself fish for these pearls, and have therefrom great profits". Don Alburquerque, Governor of India, visited Bahrain in 1514 and noted its pearl fisheries with envy, claiming that they were superior to those elsewhere in the Gulf. On his return to Hormuz the following year he ordered from Bahrain many of the pearls which were required by the King of Portugal.

But of all the tales about the Bahrain pearl fisheries by far the most bizarre is a report by a European traveller writing in 1638 A.D. He stated that Bahraini pearl divers used a form of diving helmet made from oiled leather, connected to the surface by pipes. Laws passed in Bahrain and Saudi Arabia forbade the use of diving suits, their aim being to give everyone an equal chance to fish without the richer merchants gaining an unfair advantage by the use of mechanical equipment. It is strange therefore that in the 17th century, when severe penalties were in force for those pearlers caught using diving suits, one writer at least observed that the rules were not always strictly obeyed.

1 - Koran 17:23; 22:33; 27:24.

Moving ahead to the 18th century, we have already learnt that it was the presence of the pearl fisheries of Bahrain that attracted the Al-Khalifa family from Kuwait, first to Zubara and then after their victory over the Persians, to Bahrain. It is therefore worth pausing to reflect just how this profitable trade operated. The centre of this ancient industry was a 700 mile (1167 kms) embankment in the Gulf from Ras al-Misha'ab, south of Kuwait, to Ras al-Khaimah, one of the Northern Emirates. Pearl-bearing oysters were found in most of the Gulf in depths varying from the low water-mark to twenty fathoms, the most productive beds being north and east of Bahrain's islands. The tradition was that the Kuwait fleet moved south when the Bahrain fleet moved north. None of the beds were charted and occasionally they shifted. Sometimes the divers would reap a fine harvest; at other times their diving grounds were sterile. Although it is said that Bahrain captured ninety percent of the pearl trade, it was nevertheless a hard and dangerous life for the divers, especially as the Arabs believed that the finest, purest and whitest pearls came from the deep water and no artificial diving equipment was used.

One of the most fascinating accounts of what this entailed was written by Sir Charles Belgrave when he joined a pearling expedition some fifty years ago.

"The diving season[1] lasted for four months and ten days from June till early October, when the sea is hot and calm. The diving dhows would return only once or twice in the season to replenish their supplies and the man in charge of the expedition, the Nakuda, would find his way anywhere in the seas around Bahrain without a compass.

"The crew of about sixty men consisted of divers, pullers who worked the diving ropes and manned the oars, a couple of ship's boys, a cook, the captain's mate and the captain himself. The divers who looked thin reduced their food to the minimum but the pullers were stalwart men with tremendous chest and arm development. The divers worked stripped ex-

1 - The Ruler of Bahrain officially proclaimed the opening and closing of the diving season, called Al-Ghaws. The opening day was called Al-Rakba.

Plate 20: Pearl Diving Expedition

cept for a loincloth or a very short pair of shorts made of dark material, any colour would attract dangerous fish. During the jelly-fish season, they wore cotton garments covering the body to avoid being stung.

"Everything on board the dhow was done to the accompaniment of singing, stamping and hand-clapping, especially when the men were at the oars. As they heaved the heavy, square-bladed oars through the water, keeping excellent time, their voices rose and then descended in a sound like a long drawn-out groan. There were two men to each oar and they rowed standing. Having pushed the heavy oar through the water, the rowers rapidly moved to the other side of the oar, pushed it back more easily as it was not in the water, then changed sides again for the next stroke. When we reached the place where the diving was to be done the anchor was lowered, the oars were lashed to the rowlocks so that they projected horizontally above the water, and diving began.

"Each diver had two ropes. One of them, on which he descended had a stone weight on it, the other was fastened to a string bag (dehyeen) into which he put his shells. On his nose he wore a clip (foota'am) and his fingers and big toes were provided with leather guards (khabat) to protect him when he walked on a sharp coral on the sea-bed and pulled oysters off the rocks.

"The puller standing on the gunwhale let down the diver on the weighted rope and then pulled it up again. The diver collected as many shells as he could, eight to twelve shells seemed to be the average number, put them in his bag and signalled to his puller who drew him up by the rope which was fastened to the bag.

"They stayed submerged for just under a minute. The captain told me that sometimes they worked banks which were twelve fathoms below the surface (72 feet) but more often they dived in about six fathoms. When the divers came alongside the pullers took the bags from them and the divers rested in the water, holding on to a rope. When all of them had surfaced, the pullers singing and stamping in unison, advanced to the heap of shells on the deck and emptied on to it the contents of the bags. After ten dives the men came on board for a rest. They drank a little coffee and huddled round the fire which burned in a fire-box on deck while another relay of divers took their places. This continued throughout the day.

"The pearl merchant's launch was the antithesis of the diving dhow. It was carpeted with Persian rugs and provided with cushions. Along the side were rolls of bedding and porous earthenware jars of water hanging on the rails. No buyer may go on to a pearling dhow while another buyer is on board, so when there was news of a big pearl being found the buyers raced to the banks to be first on the scene.

"Divers were not paid wages but shared in the profits which were obtained by the sale of the pearls. At the beginning of the season and once during the off-season they were paid an advance by their captains, which was debited against their earnings the next season. This advance payment always attracted men to the industry, but it also compelled them to work for the captain the following season."

It is therefore not surprising that whilst there were riches to be gained from the industry, the pearl divers' lot was not healthy, nor necessarily a prosperous one.

OIL INDUSTRY

We have read already the story of the discovery of oil in Bahrain, but the circumstances of its subsequent exploration would not be complete without a biographical note on the New Zealand mining engineer Frank Holmes, who earned the affectionate name "Father of Oil" and later became BAPCO's first chief local representative.

As Senior Supply Officer for the British Army during World War I in Mesopotamia, as Iraq was then called, Major Holmes had travelled extensively throughout the Arabian Gulf area. For a time he worked at the Admiralty in London, where he had access to petroleum maps. These had left him thoughtful. He was convinced that mineral and petroleum resources were hidden beneath the desert, bitumen seepages in Bahrain having given him particularly optimistic signs.

When he was in London, in 1920, Holmes persuaded a group of investors to form the Eastern and General Syndicate to seek mining and drilling concessions in the Gulf States. Successful in his objective, he was retained as their agent. Returning to the Middle East in the early 1920s, Holmes soon learned that a far more valued commodity at that time was water, and so he turned his attention to drilling water wells. In 1924 while in Bahrain he offered to drill two artesian wells with the proviso that if the venture were to fail there would be no charge; if it were to be successful, the fee would include serious consideration of Holmes' application for an oil concession. Fortune prevailed, the wells produced fresh water and a delighted Shaikh Hamed gave Holmes and his company an exclusive oil option over an area of 100,000 acres (40,500 hectares) on 2nd December 1925.

Sadly, the London investors were less than enthusiastic. They were more interested in selling the concession that Holmes had just won than in developing it. Eventually in 1927, after a two-year renewal, the Syndicate sold its option to Eastern Gulf Oil. However, on learning of a long-standing political agreement between Great Britain and Bahrain whereby any oil development would be restricted to a British company, Eastern Gulf Oil assigned its option over to Standard Oil Company of California (SOCAL). In order to give their wholly-owned subsidiary British status, SOCAL incorporated the Bahrain Petroleum Company Ltd. (BAPCO) under Canadian law on 11th January 1929.

By 14th May the following year, SOCAL's production chief, William F. Taylor, and senior geologist, Fred A. Davies[1], had arrived in Bahrain. In order to observe the surface structure of the island in relation to Jebel Dukhan, Davies walked the encircling rimrock, a distance of some 35 miles, before he decided on the site of Well Number 1. This confident conclusion was to herald the arrival of the advance drilling party on 26th May 1931, led by SOCAL's Edward A. Skinner.[2]

1 - Later BAPCO's first General Manager. Retired in 1959 as
    Chairman of ARAMCO.
2 - BAPCO's first Vice-President

Plate 21: Edward Skinner standing on Jebel Dukhan,
overlooking the Jebel Camp and the first oil well.

When at 6 o'clock in the morning of 1st June 1932 oil
began to flow at the rate of 9,600 barrels a day, Bahrain's
oil industry had began. Skinner reported that the event was
like a "real driller's dream", and although the field was small,
of the first fifty development wells drilled, only one hole was
dry.

SOCAL's immediate task was to establish a permanent camp
for the drilling teams at the foot of the Jebel Dukhan. Associated with this project was the building of a bridge from
Sitra island to the main island of Bahrain, so that supplies
from the Sitra jetty could be brought overland to the camp.
Later Awali town was created in the centre of the island
which now houses the offices and homes of the company's
employees.

In June 1934, BAPCO's first cargo of crude oil was loaded at
the Sitra Terminal and on 29th December Shaikh Hamed
granted a Mining Lease to BAPCO which covered an area of

approximately 100,000 acres of Bahrain's main island. Later negotiations resulted in the lease being varied so that at one time it covered all Bahrain's land and offshore area.

The following year saw work commence on the refinery. The original idea was that refined petroleum products would be marketed to the United States, but the small initial 10,800 barrels a day crude oil distillation unit soon proved inadequate. Rapid expansion of the plant continued until a refining capacity of 255,000 barrels a day was reached in 1978.

However, mindful of the diminishing oil-field reserves, the company subsequently reduced its crude oil production in order to conserve stocks, so that nowadays only a quarter of the through-put comes from the Bahrain field. The remaining three-quarters is brought across from Saudi Arabia by means of a 200,000 barrels a day pipeline traversing a total of 55 kilometres of sea-bed and desert.

On 30th June 1936, California Texas Oil Company Ltd. (CALTEX) came into being, with the Bahrain Petroleum Company as the principal operating company of the Caltex Group. Over the subsequent years more than three hundred wells have been drilled for oil and gas exploration, giving a cumulative total of oil produced since 1932 as at 31st December 1979 of 671,999,683 barrels (the latest published figure).

A milestone in BAPCO's half-century association with the Bahrain government was the initialling of a participation agreement on 15th December 1979, under which the Government would acquire sixty percent of BAPCO's interests in the refinery. The signing of this agreement took place on 19th July 1980, and on 4th May 1981 this was formalised with the signing of the Memorandum and Articles of Association at Government House, whereby the Government became the majority shareholder of the refinery, with CALTEX retaining a forty percent interest in the newly-incorporated Bahrain Petroleum Company B.S.C. (Closed).[1]

1 - B.S.C. (Closed -   Bahrain Stock Company, the shares of which are held privately and are not available to the public.

Plate 22: BANAGAS Plant

GAS INDUSTRY

At present over 350 million cubic feet of non-associated gas are produced daily from the Khuff zone, 200 c.f.d. of which is used by the oil industry, 100 c.f.d. by the aluminium smelter and 50 c.f.d. for power generation. Over the next ten years, demand, largely due to the increase in power generation requirements, is scheduled to rise to 500 million c.f.d. At this rapid rate of consumption it is estimated that the Khuff reserves will last for a further forty-five years, but in terms of future planning Mr. Yusif Al-Shirawi Bahrain's present Minister of Development and Industry reported in mid-1981 that this was an "uncomfortably narrow margin".

However, gas exploration is still very much in its infancy, not only in Bahrain but in the Gulf area as a whole. As a result, BANOCO (Bahrain National Oil Company) proposes to investigate further exploitation potential in two or three years by embarking on a series of deep test drillings to the "basement" of the field, thought to lie at around 17,000 feet. As this is some five or six thousand feet beyond the Khuff zone depth of 11,000 to 12,000 feet, it is widely hoped that this will prove as resourceful as the early "wildcat" oil holes of fifty years ago.

MARKETS - OLD AND NEW

Traditional markets in Arab towns have the same general characteristics. Producers and retailers of the same goods occupy adjacent stalls and each trade has a lane of its own. The 20th century Arab geographer Yaqut insists that there are "two indispensable qualifications of (Moslem) urban life: a Friday mosque and a market place" (see Route 3).

Another contemporary writer states, "It is altogether fitting that a permanent market should be regarded an essential element of the Moslem town which came into being to serve the function of trade. The order in which trades followed one another in the layout of the markets was substantially the same. Near the mosque, the religious centre, were the suppliers of the sanctuary, the intellectual centre (the suq of the booksellers and book binders, principally for the sale of the Koran) and the shoe makers, all of which used the same raw material: leather.

Plate 23: Old Fruit and vegetable Market

"Adjoining this group of markets was the covered textile suq
which was lockable and which for this reason also housed the
shops and stores of the precious commodities. Next to the
textile trade came the carpenters, locksmiths and the craftsmen, and at the edge of the central zone were the temporary
markets, where perishable goods and handicrafts supplied by
the agricultural hinterland were sold. Here too were the
stalls of the basketmakers and other industries such as the
potters, located on the edge of the city limits.

"In the new towns the merchants would sit cross-legged in
their small square shops surrounded by their goods stacked
high about them. The whole image endowed these towns
with a unique sense of place which, fortunately, we are
still able to enjoy in the few surviving markets of the Moslem
world".

Usam Ghaidam, a UNESCO architect, who has studied amongst other suqs those in Doha (Qatar) and Deira (Dubai), could
well have been writing of Bahrain, for the *Manama Suq* of
today, apart from the fact that it is not covered, presents very

56

Plate 24: Candy Store, Manama Suq

much the same picture. In Route 3, we pass the Friday Mosque on Al-Khalifa Road, and continue along the old shore-line to the lanes which border on the market, with the cloth and gold suqs in its centre. The *Muharraq Suq*, although considerably smaller, is similar in concept (see Route 1). However, during the 1970s, increasing traffic congestion and cramped food storage facilities made it necessary for a new *Central Market* to be constructed for the sale of perishable foods. Some traders, fearing that traditions, "the sense of place" and their livelihoods would disappear, resisted the move. However, by 1978 when the new fish, meat, fruit and vegetable markets were opened adjacent to King Faisal Highway, it was clear that the new covered premises would provide much better trading facilities than previously. Although the market is only three years old, it would seem to all outward appearances that the thriving, colourful markets of the old suq have re-established themselves quite successfully. With the imminent completion of a new mosque beside this complex, the two indispensable requirements of Moslem urban life (according .to Yaqut) will consolidate the entry of this modern new centre (see Route 3).

57

By the end of 1981 the new **Muharraq Central Market** will have opened to cater for wholesale and retail buyers in the area, principally to provide air-conditioning for fish, meat and vegetables. Plans are under way to open another similar central market on reclaimed land in Muharraq in 1983.

Two temporary open-air markets, the Wednesday and Thursday markets, operated in Bahrain until quite recently. As their names suggest, they were held on specific days of the week when traders brought their goods from the country to be sold in the town.

Plate 25: Suq Al-Khamis, 1934

The **Wednesday Market** still exists in a limited form on the edge of the Manama Suq (marked on the Route 3 map). It is possible to see items such as pottery from Aali village (Route 5), embroidered thobes and model dhows on sale.

The **Thursday Market**, known locally as the **Suq Al-Khamis,** was located on a site still evident today on Route 5, adjacent to the Mosque which bears the same name. It is no coincidence that once again the two essential components of Moslem urban life present themselves at this particular place, for in the Middle Ages Bahrain's capital town, Bilad Al-Qadim, was situated just south-east of the Mosque on what was then coast. Although the old city is now in ruins and a major highway separates the Mosque from the present Al-Khamis district, it was to this market-place beside a place of prayer that the villagers from the south, east and west brought their wares. Even after the development of Manama, but prior to the tarmac road construction and availability of motorised transport, Suq Al-Khamis remained a more convenient and active weekly market for those who had to travel some distance from the outlying illages. The photograph (Plate 25) taken almost fifty years ago shows the scene of livestock trading quite clearly. It was not until the early 1960s that the market ceased to function.

We now turn our attention to the 20th century, and the phenomenon of international **money markets**. As part of Bahrain's programme of diversification during the last decade, the island state has established itself as a leading banking centre in the Middle East, dominated by over sixty offshore banking units, (OBUs).[1] These began to appear in 1975 with the aim of attracting the cash surplus of the neighbouring oil states for investment in money market and foreign exchange transactions. However, this would not have been possible without the complementary rapid development of the telecommunications industry. As manifestation of its importance, Bahrain's offshore banks reported profits of $191 million in 1980[2], with an increase of 12.5% in the following six months to an asset total of $42.9 billion by the end of June 1981.

1 - By 31st October 1981, the Bahrain Monetary Agency had issued 67 OBU licences.

2 - At this time there were 58 licenced offshore banking units (OBUs).

Hallmarks for gold:
above, 18 carat; below, 21 carat.

Hallmarks for silver:
above, 95.84 per cent silver; below, 92.5 per cent silver.

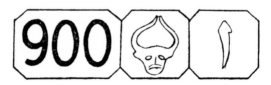

The Bahrain Monetary Agency (the Central Bank) is also keen to develop Bahrain as a *gold market*. As a preliminary to this, a new hallmarking law was enforced in August 1980, designed to protect customers and traders. It had taken four years of training and negotiation with the London Assay Office to draw up the Law, at a cost of BD. 35,000 in equipment. The gold hallmark, covering items over 18 carats in value, bears the national flag; the silver hallmark, a bull's head, covers items with a silver content exceeding 92.5%. As a tentative start to commodity trading, 8 precious metals and commodity dealing licences have been issued; these are regarded as just the beginning of what is hoped will become an international *bullion market*, centered in Bahrain.

Mina Manama

Qalaat Al-Bahrain aerial shot

PART II: THEMATIC GUIDE

5. ARCHAEOLOGICAL SITES

FLINT SITES

During the course of the Danish Expedition's survey of the southern part of Bahrain during the 1950s, a number of flint sites were discovered in the south-western desert stretches. Worked flints were found where the wind had uncovered the ancient ground surface which in most of the coastal areas had been covered by a metre or more of sand. Professor P.V. Glob, who conducted the survey, concluded that an absolute date for the oldest artefacts which belong to Bahrain's Old Stone Age cannot be given as yet, "but at a reasonable estimate the dating would appear to lie between 50,000 and 20,000 years ago".

The majority of flints bear similar cultural characteristics to those just mentioned but are of a later date. "They consist almost entirely of rough flakes and chips, as well as cores with various degrees of flaking. Regular blades are scarcely ever found, only some few struck with a blow from the side and not, as is usually the case, from the end. The main impression given by the specimens collected, is that they belong to the Middle Palaeolithic flake culture" (c. 8000-7000 B.C.).

Professor Glob suggests that a great number of worked cores and chips of the Bahrain flints closely resemble the Sohan culture of India, the settlements of which lie thickly in a series of river valleys in north-west Punjab. He also believes that a late Palaeolithic date (c. 7000-6000 B.C.) may be ascribed to certain arrowheads which are fashioned from pointed blades with the tangs flaked from the front. It is possible that these arrowheads, utilised for hunting, are contemporary with an early agricultural economy based on crop growing, evidence for which is indicated by the discovery of a series of toothed sickle blades.

Seven years ago in late 1974, John Clingly (former headmaster of Awali School) visited the Howar Islands (see map preceding page 1) where he discovered a flint site covering approximately one hundred square metres. From his study it appeared that the flints were imported from the nearby Qatar peninsula in antiquity since the type is not indigenous to either the Howar island group or to Bahrain. This would help to explain why the incidence of arrow heads and scrapers is not prolific and their quality poor when compared with those flints found elsewhere on Bahrain island.

None of the flint sites are visited specifically in Part III, the Location Guide, although reference is made to some of them in Route 6. The Howar Islands may be reached by boat, an outward journey of at least two hours depending upon the vessel and the sea state. Visitors who are unfamiliar with Bahrain's coastal waters and climatic conditions are cautioned from embarking on an expedition without adequate preparation. At the very least the boat should be equipped with a compass, reserve fuel and fresh drinking water, life-jackets and distress flares. It is wise to inform the Coastguard Base in Muharraq of your destination and estimated time of return.

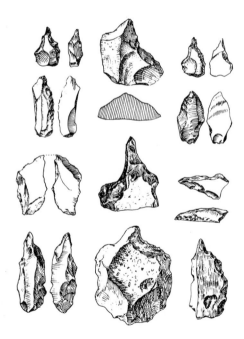

Plate 26: Flints

TUMULI AND SETTLEMENT EXCAVATIONS

Serious interest in the concealed heritage of Bahrain was first expressed with considerable enthusiasm during the latter part of the nineteenth century. The fascination which drew early travellers to the village of Aali (see Route 5) was a collection of vast burial mounds which, in size, represented the largest of the estimated 100,000 tumuli on Bahrain island. Because of its immense dimensions, this Aali group was later called the Royal Burial Mounds.

Subsequently many other sites have been excavated, which apart from the flints already mentioned have produced evidence of differing burial customs, fortifications, temples and domestic buildings.

Tumuli are evident to the greatest extent in the west region of Bahrain island along a north-south axis (Route 7). In general they are situated above the ten metre contour whereas the settlement areas are usually located below it. Since natural spring water sources frequently rise between the two, it is probable that the choice of high ground for the mounds was to ensure that the graves remained dry, whilst the settlements could be assured of a constant flow of water by being at a lower level. The widest spread of burial mounds occurred in the Barbar period with the Seleucid and Parthian periods being well represented (see chapter 6).

Tumuli excavations conducted during 1981 at West Rifaa (near to the Bahrain Defence Force Hospital) have exposed tombs which are considered as the oldest yet to have been discovered on the island. Although the excavation report is yet to be completed, it is believed that pottery found at this site is probably contemporary with that identified at Jebel Hafit (Abu Dhabi) dated to c. 3,000 - 2,800 B.C. Current rescue excavations at Saar have produced a new type of burial complex attributed to the Dilmun civilisation, similar in age but not in type to the majority of tumuli graves in Bahrain.

Unfortunately, many of the Rifaa and Saar mounds will be destroyed during the next few years as a result of the construction of a new town centred on Buri village and the completion of the eastern extremity of the Bahrain-Saudi

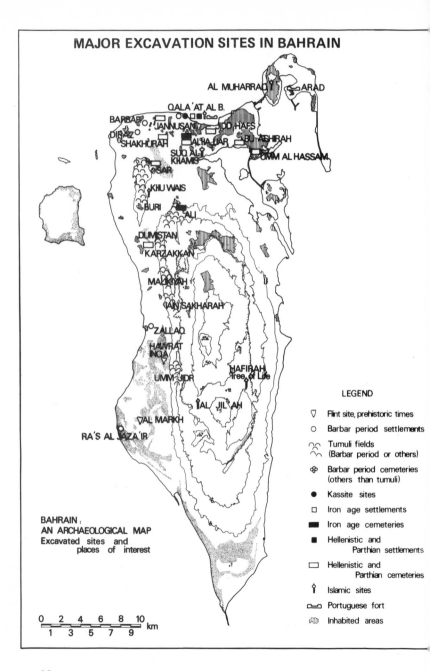

MAJOR EXCAVATION SITES IN BAHRAIN

AL MUHARRAD ⚊ ARAD

QALA´AT AL B.

BARBAR

DIRAZ

JANNUSAN

JIDD HAFS

SHAKHURAH

AL HAJAR

ABU ASHIRAH

SUQ AL

KHAMIS

UMM AL HASSAM

SAR

KHU WAIS

BURI

ALI

DUMISTAN

KARZAKKAN

MALKIYAH

AIN SAKHARAH

ZALLAQ

HAWRAT

INDA

UMM JIDR

HAFIRAH
Tree of Life

AL JIL AH

AL MARKH

RA´S AL JAZA´IR

LEGEND

▽   Flint site, prehistoric times

○   Barbar period settlements

⌢⌢   Tumuli fields
⌢⌢   (Barbar period or others)

⊕   Barbar period cemeteries
    (others than tumuli)

●   Kassite sites

□   Iron age settlements

■   Iron age cemeteries

■   Hellenistic and
    Parthian settlements

▭   Hellenistic and
    Parthian cemeteries

⚲   Islamic sites

⌐⌐   Portuguese fort

⊞   Inhabited areas

BAHRAIN :
AN ARCHAEOLOGICAL MAP
Excavated sites and
    places of interest

0   2   4   6   8   10
                        km
  1   3   5   7   9

Arabia Causeway. However, at the time of writing, Avenue 90 (Route 7) provides an excellent vantage point from which to sight many hundred mounds and some of the current excavation work.

Other tumuli may be seen on either side of the Budaiya Highway (Route 8). Those at Al-Hajjar represent the Seleucid and Parthian periods (see chapter 6).

The excavation of fortifications, temples and domestic buildings has been given prominent attention by archaeologists during the last quarter of a century, particularly along the northern sector of Bahrain island and Muharraq. The Arad Fort (Route 2) built by the Omanis c. 1800 A.D. and the Bahrain Fort complex (Route 8), comprising an 11th century Islamic Fort and 16th century Portuguese Fort, have been investigated extensively by Danish and French expeditions. Work will continue at the Islamic Fort during the 1981 winter season.

Plate 27: Arad Fort

The triple-temple site of Barbar, the colonnaded temple of Diraz and the well-temple of Umm Es-Sujur are unique examples of religious architecture of the pre-Islamic periods (see Route 8).

Many of the settlement excavations have been back-filled in order to preserve the remains. However, sections of monumental city walls and domestic architecture representing five occupation levels attributed to the last three millennia B.C. are evident on the Bahrain Fort (Qalaat Al-Bahrain) tell (city-mound).

Those readers who are interested in excavations not mentioned in this chapter may refer to the list of excavations which appears in Part IV together with the bibliography which includes references to most of the relevant excavation reports.

Plate 28: Altar, Diraz Temple

TUMULI CONSTRUCTION FEATURES

It is generally agreed that there are over 100,000 burial mounds dispersed throughout the northern segment of Bahrain. An unconfirmed recent estimate places the figure closer to 150,000. Whichever figure one chooses to believe, their construction represents an incredible task for the builders, who had no mechanical equipment, just flint and bronze tools.

Often called **Muraqib** by the local people, the majority of the mounds are conical in shape with rounded apices. Some of these have been flattened through disturbance, usually robberies in antiquity. They range from 26 feet (8 m.) to 80 feet (24.5 m.) high and 18 feet (5.5 m.) to 100 feet (30.5 m.) in diameter. Excavation during the last century has produced a wide range of tombs and burials, the latter usually being positioned in an east-west orientation. Artefacts recovered from these graves include such burial matter as gold, jewellery, bronze weapons and bitumen covered baskets.

Single chamber tombs usually have a west entrance flanked on each side by a supporting column of walling and capped with large stones. The entrance was closed by smaller stones, with larger ones at the base arranged as a doorstep. The wall construction comprised approximately five courses of drystone walling of roughly-fashioned local limestone whilst the roof was formed by four or five massive stone slabs. Frequently the floor was bed rock. Often an alcove was built at the east end into the northern wall and roofed with a single large stone (see Fig. 3).

Plate 29 : Single-storey burial chamber

Double-Chambered Tombs were first discovered by the late nineteenth century excavators at Aali village where the tumuli are often referred to as the "Royal" mounds due to their exceptional size. Examples of double-tombs have since been excavated at Janabiya, Kuraiya and Saar. Normally, one chamber is placed immediately above the other, both being rectangular, aligned east-west, with alcoves at the eastern corners and often at the western corners also.

Like the single tombs, the chambers are built of dry stone walling, plastered with gypsum on the inside, and roofed with enormous limestone capstones. The walls of the lower chamber stand vertically while those of the upper chamber usually incline slightly at the top. The size of the chambers varies considerably, some as much as 40 feet in length, 18 feet in height and 6 feet in width. The west entrances were sealed after the burial had been placed inside, and a vertical retaining wall of stone blocks was then constructed to surround the mound. (see Fig. 3).

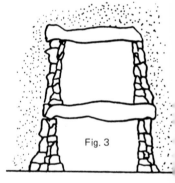

Multiple Chambers excavated in the Al-Hajjar complex fill a gap in the burial history of Bahrain between the Bronze Age of the third millennium B.C. and the Hellenistic period up to the 3rd century A.D. These graves are unique since steps descend into them which over the years have been altered or added to. Walls built within the entrances in later periods still stand. Pottery found at Al-Hajjar is ascribed to the Kassite and Assyrian phases.

Fig. 3

Double Graves are unusual, but a Hellenistic example was discovered during rescue excavations at Umm Al-Hassam on the site of the present Moon Plaza supermarket (not included in the routes in this guide). In this case, two skeletons lay side by side, denoting perhaps a married couple.

Rock Chambers have been excavated during the last quarter century, comprising a selection of fascinating features. During a rescue dig at Abu Ashira, near Umm Al-Hassam during the 1970s, a chamber with a sloping ramp was discovered. The ramp had been carved through a rock and led down to a three-sided chamber containing a platform and niches to receive bodies. In the centre of the chamber there was a column base. Another new feature discovered during this rescue dig was the presence of hearths which still contained ashes. These probably served as receptacles for ceremonial funeral rites.

Conical rock tombs have been discovered on the island of Umm An-Nassan, and a recent excavation in the south of Bahrain at Umm Jidr revealed rock chambers constructed in a parallel sequence (see Fig. 4).

W NW   c   b   a   E. SE

UMM JIDR tomb 1   Fig. 4

Grave Complexes are a comparatively recent discovery, but equally important, as excavations at Saar have revealed. Here a central burial is often flanked by secondary burials around the perimeter of the main tumulus (see Plate 30).

Plate 30: Secondary burials (see Route 7)

6. ARTEFACTS

After nearly a century of archaeological investigation on the islands of Bahrain, a wealth of material has been excavated which has contributed significantly to the nation's heritage and to the study of the islands' history.

Four major categories of artefacts are highlighted in this chapter, namely pottery, seal-stones, statuary and glassware, although the minor classifications are worthy of a preliminary mention.

Limited examples of ivory pieces were excavated at various sites, one in particular being the torso of a small statue together with circular ivory boxes in the tumuli at Aali. Ostrich shells fashioned as drinking vessels were not restricted to isolated burials, indicating that these birds may have been native to the islands at least in the third and fourth millennia B.C. An alabaster mace-head and bowls containing snake-burials were found at Barbar and Qalaat Al-Bahrain respectively. Jewellery and a silver coin hoard were also found at Qalaat Al-Bahrain.

POTTERY may be divided into distinct categories, which are summarised as follows:

Ubaid Pottery	4th millennium B.C.		
Barbar Ware	2,800 B.C. -	1,800	B.C.
Kassite Ware	1,600 B.C. -	1,100	B.C.
Assyrian Ware	850 B.C. -	650	B.C.
Neo-Babylonian Ware	650 B.C. -	500	B.C.
Classical or Seleucid Ware	300 B.C. -	150	B.C.
Hellenistic or Parthian Ware	150 B.C. -	300	A.D.
Mediaeval or Islamic Ware	800 A.D. -	1,600	A.D.
Late Ware	1,600 A.D. -		

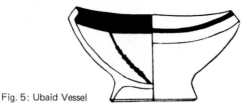

Fig. 5: Ubaid Vessel

It is inevitable that scholars' opinions differ on the subject of archaeological interpretation, and therefore the foregoing table and the following summary should be taken as a guide and not a definitive analysis.

The *Ubaid culture*, named after its type-site near the Euphrates River in Southern Iraq (Mesopotamia) is believed to have lasted from 6,000 - 4,000 B.C. Professor David Oates of the University of London located pottery along the Arabian Gulf attributed to phases of this culture. Almost forty sites in Saudi Arabia, two in Bahrain (Al-Markh and Diraz) and four in Qatar have yielded painted Ubaid sherds or post-Ubaid sherds at sites which have been dated to between 5,000 and 3,700 B.C.

Apart from Ubaid pottery found at Al-Markh and Diraz the earliest pottery found in Bahrain is that from City I at Qalaat Al-Bahrain which included chain-ridged *Barbar ware*. The date of this pottery has been disputed, but at the earliest it is not likely to be before 3,000 B.C. and more probably c. 2,500 B.C.

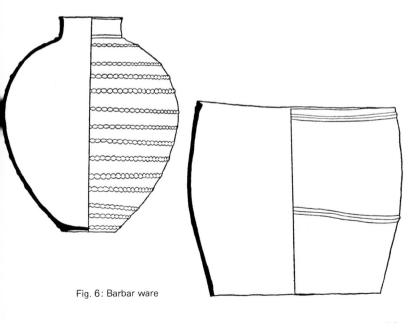

Fig. 6: Barbar ware

Two major pottery types represent the City II levels at Qalaat Al-Bahrain and the Barbar Temple. It is very recognisable and uniform, comprising large vessels the size of pumpkins, shaped like eggs in red clay and decorated with horizontal ridges usually a centimetre apart.

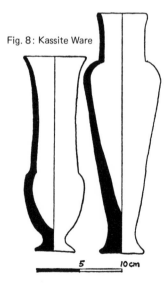

Fig. 7: City II Pottery

5cm   10cm

Kassite Ware of the type excavated along the north coast of Bahrain (Qalaat Al-Bahrain and Al-Hajjar) is referred to by some archaeologists as "caramel ware". The greatest number of sherds belong to tall drinking vessels with funnel-shaped necks and narrow solid bases which develop into regular pedestals.

Plate 31: Kassite ware on display at the National Museum

Fig. 8: Kassite Ware

5   10cm

The Kassite tribe filtered into Babylonia from the fringes of the Zagros Mountains. They assumed power in 1595 B.C. filling a vacuum which had been created by Hittite attacks ending the reigning dynasty. Until the Kassites were overwhelmed by the Elamites in 1157 B.C., a type of pottery known as Kassite Ware was in use throughout Southern Mesopotamia.

The bowls of the *Classical or Seleucid period* are characterised by their burnished appearance. They range in size from 5 to 13 centimetres and 13 to 23 centimetres in diameter. Common to all of them was that their bases were either flat or furnished with three stub feet.

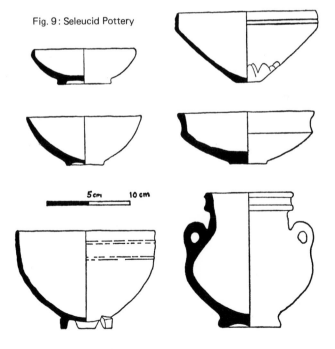

Fig. 9 : Seleucid Pottery

5 cm   10 cm

The following illustrations of **Medieval or Islamic Ware** represent a few of the vessels which are attributed to this period.

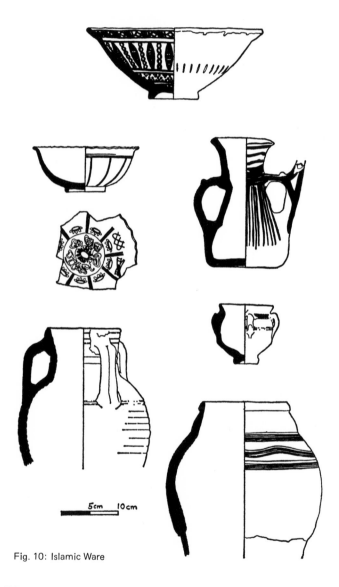

Fig. 10: Islamic Ware

SEAL STONES were prolific in the Mesopotamian and Indus valley cultures. Usually made of steatite (soapstone), with an incised design on one flat surface, they were used to make impressions in soft clay or wax, representing a signature or mark of ownership. Early excavation in Bahrain demonstrated that the southern shores of the Arabian Gulf did not reflect the same trend. However, the subsequent discovery of fifty round stamp seals in the Barbar Temples and the City I and II levels at Qalaat Al-Bahrain was exciting not only because of their very presence, but because they demonstrated a type and age which was clearly foreign to the cylinder seals of Mesopotamia and the square seals of the Indus valley. Geoffrey Bibby's find of the remains of a seal-carver's workshop showed beyond doubt that at least some of the seals originated in Bahrain.

The most notable sites of discovery were the Al-Hajjar Kassite graves (c. 1,800 - 1,200 B.C.) and the Temples of Barbar and Diraz, where the seals date to c. 2,400 B.C. Unpublished examples have been excavated in recent years at the Umm Jidr and Saar sites. The earliest and most primitive examples date from around 3,000 B.C. The display in the National Museum shows clearly the development of the designs.

Many of the circular stamp seals are of a uniform type. Among the features etched into their tiny proportions (some are barely 10 mm. in diameter) are an opposed warrior armed with spear and shield, a quadruped with a head resembling that of a cock and three smaller figures including a scorpion and a gazelle rampant.

Plate 32:
Seal-stone impression

STATUARY has been one of the most impressive classifications of artefact to be excavated at the temple sites of Bahrain. Although finds have been limited so far they are of a particularly fine quality. A headless limestone statue (21 cms. high) was discovered on the staircase leading to the well-chamber of the Ain Umm Es-Sujur (Route 8) and another (20 cms. high) in the chamber itself. Both were of roughly carved stone, apparently quarried on Jidda island. Unfortunately, the heads have not been found, although the torsos are on display in the National Museum.

The entrance to the "well-temple" of the three superimposed Barbar Temples and the chamber of the Diraz Temple enclosure were flanked by cult objects or statues which are thought to have borne a direct connection with ritual acts or ceremonial cleansings.

A bull's head, 20 cms. high and cast in the round (Plate 33) lay in the corner of a room Temple II at Barbar, together with a heap of copper bands. The eyes were originally inlaid. Two other copper figurines of a naked, clean-shaven man in the posture of supplication and a bird (all of which are in the Museum - Route 2) were excavated at the site.

Plate 33:
Bull's head
excavated at Barbar

GLASSWARE has been found in very limited quantities, but some of the examples which were excavated at the Al-Hajjar, Ash-Shakhoura, Umm Al-Hassam and Abu Ashira Hellenistic sites, together with those Islamic examples from the fort of the same period at Qalaat Al-Bahrain, are on display in a single showcase in the Museum.

Plate 34: Glass artefacts on display in the National Museum

7. TRADITIONAL ARCHITECTURE

PALACES AND HOUSES

The oldest houses in Bahrain date only from the early nineteenth century, but their style of construction is thought to have developed three to four hundred years earlier. The style has certain general affinities with the architecture of the rest of the Arabian Gulf area, including Persia (Iran), but it is essentially unique to Bahrain.

The main consideration in the construction of dwellings, apart from the raw materials available, is always climate. In the Arabian Gulf, hot and humid summers alternate with cool winters characterised by strong winds. Structures have to be sturdy and provide good shelter, but they also have to be as cool as possible for most of the year. Nowadays air-conditioning has helped to alleviate the climatic problem, but the considerations of adapting building materials to suit the rigorous demands of the weather remain.

Plate 35: Traditional House, Bahrain

Rubble (hasa) and rough pieces of local stone, often combined with coral rock (faroush) obtained from the sea, were the main building materials employed in early house construction. The latter is porous and does not hold the heat to the same extent as a denser material. The coral rock was quarried in thin slabs for use as partition walls. Wood was used to strengthen the structure whilst gypsum plaster (jus) was applied to bind and coat the walls. Typically, the houses were constructed around a central courtyard with rooms facing inwards.

The traditional houses were designed to create cool living conditions. The type of construction seen in Bahrain is sometimes called *"pier and panel"* or frame and panel. It consists of solid rubble pillars strengthened by poles with horizontal tie-beams providing further support to prevent the pillars deflecting. The intervals between the pillars provided space for shuttered windows, storage recesses or shelves. An alternative was to enclose the intervals with panelling.

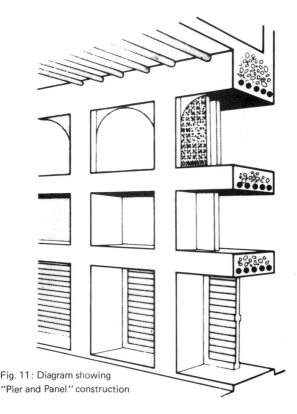

Fig. 11: Diagram showing "Pier and Panel" construction

Bait Shaikh Isa (Route 1) demonstrates this feature, particularly in Court A. Shaikh Isa's private apartments on the ground floor incorporate wall recesses similar to those just mentioned.

The piers and tie beams formed a chequer-board of recesses which were infilled according to taste. This took several characteristic forms. Frequently the lower level (register) of apertures in the reception room (majlis) was enclosed with unglazed windows which were either barred on the exterior or screened by ornamental stucco or wood carving. Not only did this feature provide a decorative facade to the house but it also allowed the passage of light and air, but not direct sunlight. The exterior of Siyadi House (Route 1) demonstrates this particularly well (see Plate 36).

Plate 36: Siyadi House

Plate 37: Barred windows

The **unglazed window casements** (derisha) were enclosed from the inside by wooden shutters which were either left plain or decoratively carved. In the case of one of the smaller rooms in the Siyadi House majlis (Route 1) the shuttered windows are faced with mirrors and the exterior of the recesses are ornamented with a geometric wooden design.

Another evident example is in Bait Shaikh Isa (Route 1) where the children's summer living quarters (room 38 on the first-floor plan) remain remarkably cool throughout the heat of the day simply by the application of derisha along the lowest register of the walls and exterior screens.

Plate 38: Lower, smaller chamber of Siyadi House double-storeyed majlis

The middle register of recesses (rawshina) was sometimes enclosed with a wall panel so that the interior niche provided display or storage space, whilst the upper register was often closed by stucco screens (naqsha). This method of construction produced tall, light buildings with walls of minimum mass thus eliminating heat retention as far as possible.

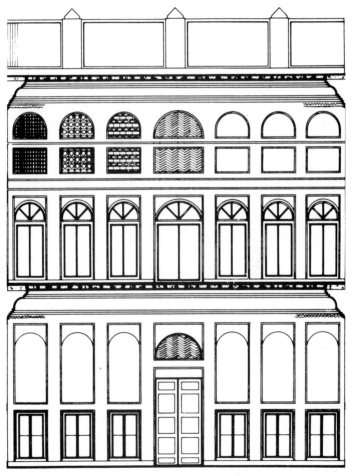

Fig. 12: Diagram to show the lower, middle and upper registers of house decoration

Plate 39: Roof and ceiling detail

Flat roofs are fairly conventional throughout the Arabian Gulf. However, the method of their construction incorporates some distinctive local variations. Wooden poles of tamarisk (ithil) or mangrove (danche), often treated with bitumen, were laid from wall to wall to provide a basic frame which was covered with palmleaf matting (jareed). This was subsequently sealed externally with a layer of mud, pebbles and plaster. Internally, ceilings were painted in decorative patterns with strong bright colours.

Another distinctive construction feature was the inclusion of specific cooling devices such as **wind towers** and **wind traps** (see chapter 10 - Engineering).

Plate 40: Windtower

Plate 41: Former residence of Al-Madder family, Muharraq (now demolished)

PALM-FROND SHELTERS (BARASTIS)

Whilst the oldest houses of Bahrain are less than two hundred years old, the custom of building dwellings with palm-fronds is a centuries-old tradition. Nowadays this method is used almost entirely for small shelters in rural areas, particularly for work areas and stores. The basket weavers of Karbabad and the fabric weavers of Bani Jamra (both referred to in Route 8) conduct their "cottage industries" within such structures.

Formerly, town-dwelling Bahrainis who owned a country estate or garden often constructed barasti houses within such confines so that the families could escape from the hot, airless weather of the urban areas. In the days before air-conditioning became available, the shelters provided shaded homes, cooled by breezes passing through the fronds. They were also remarkably sturdy and cheap to make.

The archaeologists' camp on the ramparts of Qalaat Al-Bahrain (Route 8) is a collection of dwellings of this type constructed for the Danish expedition in 1956. It is a tribute to their durability that this same camp was occupied by an archeological expedition more than twenty years later during the 1977-8 season. Geoffrey Bibby wrote: "The actual construction of the barastis was simple in theory and complex in execution. Not a single nail went into the building of the entire camp. But over a hundredweight of cord was used. First the framework of the long building was set up, with poles ten feet (3 metres) long standing vertically, one metre apart (3¼ feet), with a third of their length rammed securely into holes in the ground. A row of longer poles, two metres apart (6½ feet), ran down the centre of the building. To the tops of these vertical supports poles were lashed horizontally to form the eaves and the ridge-pole of the peaked roof, with further poles sloping up from the eaves to the ridge-pole, all lashed together to form a rigid structure.

"Then came the turn of the inner ribs of the palm leaves. These were set vertically in the ground, about five inches apart (12.7 cms.), between the poles, except where the doors were left, and tied to the eave poles and then more ribs were attached horizontally at the same interval, tied to the poles and to the vertical ribs at each point where they crossed. The

Plate 42: Barasti camp used by archaeologists, Portuguese Fort ramparts

side walls, the end walls, the eight partition walls, and the roof
were all filled in with this neat trellis-work of naked ribs, the
work going forward with incredible speed. And then the
trellis was thatched. Bundles of palm leaves were painstakingly sewn on to the supporting ribs. One of the three
old men prepared the bundles with a toothed iron sickle, and
the other two placed them in position, one standing on either
side of the wall and passing the cord back and forth on a large
wooden needle made on the spot from a length of palm-rib.
Thus the walls were filled in; the roof went even quicker. It
was formed of two layers of plaited palm-leaf mats with a
thick layer of banana leaves between."[1]

1 - Bibby, G. - Looking for Dilmun, P. 102.

MOSQUES

The mosque is the most prominent example of the types of Islamic architecture which include the fort, the palace, suq (bazaar), madrasah (school), hammam (public baths) and fountain, all of which are represented in Bahrain.

There is no standardised or basic plan determining the relevant positions or the proportions of the component structures of a mosque, nor a preference for building material. Forms of domes, arches and minarets vary greatly throughout Bahrain, as well as throughout the Islamic world. However, the following features appear in all mosques: the sahn (a courtyard where the fountain for ablution is placed); the sanctuary or sheltered area with the mihrab (a niche in a wall indicating the direction of Mecca); the mimbar (elevated

Plate 43: Halat An-Naim Mosque (minaret now demolished)

pulpit) of the Imam (the leader of the congregation) and the minaret from where the muezzin calls the faithful to prayers.

The decoration of the exteriors and interiors is predominantly non-representational. Calligraphy and geometric designs are used to convey an effect appropriate to the purpose of the building, although in Bahrain this manifests itself as a comparatively late form of ornamentation. A striking example can be seen in the Al-Khalifa Road (Route 3) were the *Juma Mosque* has an imposing minaret decorated with colourful geometric designs composed of mosaics. However since this mosque was not built until the late 1930s (from the proceeds of the first oil revenues) it cannot be equated with the simpler styles of its much earlier counterparts.

Bahrain's oldest extant mosque is the *Mosque Suq Al-Khamis*, located on the Shaikh Sulman Highway (Route 5). Its foundation date is disputed but there is sufficient evidence to suggest that the first building phase may be attributed to the 7th century A.D., contemporary with the islands' conversion to Islam. Its twin minarets remain as an imposing land-mark. The rest of the mosque is now in ruins although sections were restored in 1976.

Three much later mosques of the old mud-brick type are referred to in Routes 1, 2 and 3. They represent a style which was dominant throughout the urban areas of Manama and Muharraq during the nineteenth century. The *mosque* adjacent to *Siyadi House* (Route 1) serves as a landmark for visitors locating this site (see Plate 76). *Halat An-Naim* (Route 2) is an islet south of the Arad peninsula where pearl divers used to live and attend prayers in the mosque which dominated this tiny area of land. The old minaret (see Plate 43) has now been demolished by the sahn, sanctuary, mihrab and mimbar have been restored and are being incorporated into an enlarged place of worship surrounded by a new housing project. *Mosque Ras-Rummaan* is located at the beginning of Route 1 between two modern office buildings. Before extensive land reclamation took place, the mosque was located on a headland surrounded by a pomegranate garden from which the building takes its name. The leaning minaret is one of the few surviving mud-brick examples in Manama.

Plate 44: South-west Bastion and dry moat, Portuguese Fort

FORTS

Compared with other areas of the Middle East there are few extant military installations on the islands of Bahrain. The few which have survived resemble those of the rest of the Arabian Gulf, especially in the style of bastion construction.

The *Bahrain Fort (Qalaat Al-Bahrain)* complex embraces two fortifications (Route 8). The earlier of the two which is the earliest in Bahrain is an 11th century Islamic Fort located on the sea-shore. Over the years it has been covered with a thick sand and silt deposit, although sections of the original building have been exposed as a result of current excavations. A 16th century Portuguese Fort is located on the adjacent tell. The ramparts, three surviving bastions and the remains of a fourth are surrounded by a dry moat.

Rifaa Fort was constructed in the 17th century on an escarpment which dominates the low-lying desert between the old settlement of East Rifaa and the modern town of West Rifaa located on the opposite hillside. It was in this fort that the Ruler, Shaikh Ali Al-Khalifa, was killed by his brother, Muhammad Al-Khalifa, in 1869 during a desperate attempt to seize control of the islands (Route 6).

Manama Fort (Qalaat Al-Diwan) was built in the first half of the 18th century. Originally it consisted of four round towers joined by crenellated walls. Little of the original structure remains. Nowadays the site is occupied by the Public Security Headquarters (Route 5).

Arad Fort (Route 2) is a late 18th century Omani construction. This dominates the bay between the Arad peninsula and south Muharraq. The four bastions and retaining walls still stand to their full height although sea erosion has caused some of the foundation structure to disappear.

Abu Mahur Fort (Route 4) was re-built in its present form in 1840 by Shaikh Abdulla Al-Khalifa, who was to be besieged there three years later by his great nephew Muhammad bin Khalifa. (It was the same Muhammad bin Khalifa Al-Khalifa who later killed his brother at Rifaa Fort in 1869).

MAJOR ARCHITECTURAL SITES OF BAHRAIN

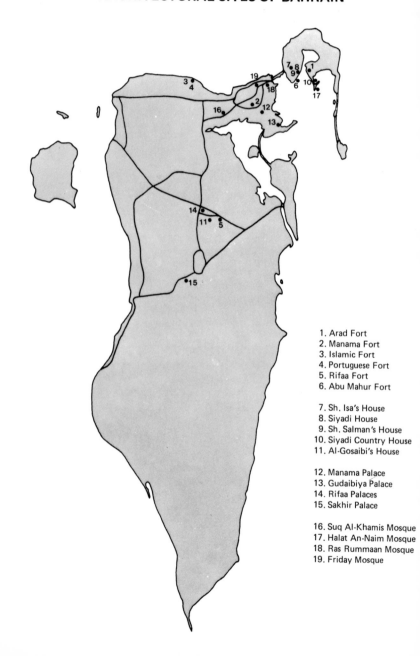

1. Arad Fort
2. Manama Fort
3. Islamic Fort
4. Portuguese Fort
5. Rifaa Fort
6. Abu Mahur Fort

7. Sh. Isa's House
8. Siyadi House
9. Sh. Salman's House
10. Siyadi Country House
11. Al-Gosaibi's House

12. Manama Palace
13. Gudaibiya Palace
14. Rifaa Palaces
15. Sakhir Palace

16. Suq Al-Khamis Mosque
17. Halat An-Naim Mosque
18. Ras Rummaan Mosque
19. Friday Mosque

8. ORNAMENTATION AND DECORATION

Ornamentation in the form of various arabesque and geometric designs and decoration was employed internally and externally in the early systems of house construction throughout the Arabian peninsula. In general, the designs were repeating patterns based on geometric symmetry and executed to accommodate local artistic taste and the individuality of the area.

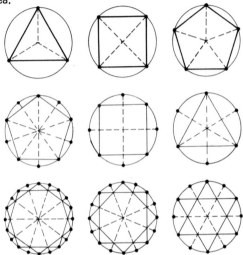

Fig. 13

Regular polygons of 3, 4, 5, 6, 8, 10, 12,16 and 20 sides obtained by joining the points of division on the circumference of a circle with straight lines.

Regular polygons sub-divided into basic units in the shape of right-angled triangles.

The triangular sub-units are equal to twice the number of sides of the comprising polygon.

In the creation of geometric patterns in traditional Islamic crafts such as wood or gypsum carving, metal, ceramic and glass designs, the compasses and ruler are the only two major instruments used. From a circle it is possible to generate any regular polygon once the circumference is divided equally into the required number of sections and straight lines join the points of the divisions. The concept of proportion is based on ratio, this being the relation between two things of the same kind of which the known measure of one is compared with that of the other, (see Figs. 13).

Throughout the Moslem world craftsmen have applied these principles to the practical creation of patterns. The method applied and developed by unknown masters is no longer a device for generating new designs, but one for reproducing the old. However, that being said, it requires considerable expertise and experience to execute these concepts in perfect harmony, especially when working with the demanding medium of fast-setting plaster which eliminates second thoughts and error correction. Four forms of ornamentation and decoration were used in Bahrain in particular: plaster ornamentation, wood carving, multicolour decoration and shaped decoration.

PLASTER AND GYPSUM ORNAMENTATION was used more frequently than any other form, such preference being attributed to the ready availability of raw materials and skilled craftsmen. Another contributing factor was the little time required for its execution.

Walls were decorated in zones and panels from the floor to the ceiling. In some cases a fret of plaster ornamentation was limited to the upper-part of the walls, and the frames of windows, doors and recessed shelves. One of the more unusual examples of extensive cut plaster ornamentation can be found in small areas around the main doorways, (see Plate 45). Such decoration projected a vitality of design, especially when the bas-relief was contrasted with dark paint to provide highlights in the white plaster.

Executing the ornamental work was a matter of covering the foundation plaster already applied to the walls with a second finer quality layer, about one centimetre in thickness. Designs were cut into the setting plaster, their complexity and extent being determined by the skill of the craftsmen.

Another method of executing plaster ornamentation was by using pre-cast, pre-ornamented panels which were created out of situ, and then fitted into place later. This method provided the facility of adjustments to aesthetic taste or mathematical misalignment.

The wall surfaces of mud houses were stengthened first with a layer of hard, light brown clay, and then covered with plaster. These designs were cut to a depth that exposed the first layer of the brown clay.

Plate 45: Entrance to the Children's Quarters, Sh. Isa's House

Plate 46: Lower, middle and upper register windows and recess ornamentation (Route 1)

Plate 47: Wooden doorway decoration, (Route 1)

MULTICOLOUR ORNAMENTATION was a popular form of house decoration used in the early systems of house construction. It was less evident from the exterior, but used extensively in house interiors, especially the public rooms, notably the majlis.

The most usual colours were red, black, blue, yellow and green, with pink being particularly popular. Not only was the paint applied to wooden window shutters and doors, but also it was used generously to decorate ceilings and the soffits of beams. This is particularly evident in the restored sections of Shaikh Isa's House and Siyadi House, (Route 1).

Plate 48: Ceiling decoration

SHAPED DECORATION was an external mode to give houses a pleasant and attractive appearance. Normally, it is seen as an integral part of external walls or as a stepped pinnacle in various forms (see Plates 49 & 50).

It was used widely in the rubble and mud houses of the early systems of house construction where the filling walls were recessed in relation to the columns. Similarly, dummy arches of different styles were employed between open columns to convey a handsome effect of shaped decoration along the length of porticos. Stepped pinnacles generally arise at the highest point of the house, such as the top of parapet walls.

Plate 49: Sakhir Palace (Route 6). Dummy arches and pinnacle decoration

Plate 50: Shaped decoration Sakhir Palace

WOODEN DOOR AND BALCONY CARVINGS in Bahrain are some of the finest extant examples of decorated woodwork in the northern areas of the Arabian Gulf. Approximately thirty of the best examples have been collected by the National Museum, two of which are on display in the Ethnography Gallery (Route 2). One of the most beautiful doorways to remain in its original location is the entrance to Siyadi House (Route 1).

Another style identified by a strictly geometric central cover strip with notches arranged in steps, appears on many doors still evident throughout Manama and Muharraq, (see Plate 52). In some cases the metal rivets which secure the wooden sections are arranged in a decorative manner and have themselves been wrought with a pattern.

Balconies were not just a function of ornamentation but also of protection for the ladies of the harem from indiscreet eyes. Plate 51 is the fine example still to be seen in Manama (marked on the map preceding Route 3). Other simpler styles, perhaps more representative, are evident in the Al-Awadiyah conservation area (see Route 5) whilst a particularly beautiful balcony may be seen at Sakhir Palace (Route 6).

Plate 51: Harem balcony, Manama

Plate 52: Doorway, Siyadi House

STAINED GLASS WINDOWS were used as a form of decoration on mud-houses (Route 3) and in the majlis of the larger houses. The favoured colours are blue, green, red and yellow, which appear as coloured glass segments in a wooden semi-circular frame above the main shuttered windows. The practical result of using coloured glass is that light is allowed to pass through yet the amount of heat entering the room is reduced.

In the case of Siyadi House (Route 1), the stained glass designs have been complemented with mirrored window shutters which reflect a kaleidoscope of colour and light (Plate 54).

Plate 53: Traditional window features

Plate 54: Interior of double majlis,
Siyadi House (Note middle and upper register recesses)

9. TRADITIONAL CRAFTS AND INDUSTRIES

DHOW BUILDING is an ancient craft, which even today has made little concession to twentieth century technology. The word dhow itself is mysterious. Some ascribe its origin to Swahili, others to an Indian corruption of the name of a Chinese ship. Lt. Commander David Howarth commented in a study he wrote on the subject, "the spelling of dhow, the initial dh, makes it look like a transcription of an Arabic word. But it is not. No Arab sailor thinks of his ship as a dhow; it is a baggala, a boom, a sambuk, a shu'ai - he has a dozen different words for different kinds of dhows". The Oxford Dictionary of Etymology traces the word back no farther than the 19th century, and no English-Arabic dictionary seen by Lt. Commander Howarth included the word at all. He therefore concluded that one has to admit that dhow is a bogus word.

However, that being said, the vessels themselves are anything but bogus. They display skilled craftsmanship which is executed from memory and with hand tools. No plans are used for their construction and all the measurements for the variations are memorised by the boat-builder. The types which can be seen in Bahrain today are the **boom**, the **sambuk**, the **shu'ai** and the **jalibut**. Other variations may be seen occasionally, such as the little inshore fishing vessel about 3 metres in length, the **shasha**, but they are less usual.

The **boom**[1] is a large ocean-going passenger and cargo vessel, many of which can be seen tied up in Mina Manama. The **sambuk**[2] was used principally for pearl-diving expeditions. Although smaller than the boom, it was constructed to withstand rough waters and long periods away from harbour. **Shu'ai** vessels up to 50 metres (164 feet) are smaller, similar ships, but usually restricted to coastal waters for local transport or for fishing. **The jalibut** is another coastal trading vessel, originally used for pearl-diving and distinguished by its vertical stem. Its length varies between 15 and 30 metres (49 and 99 feet).

---

1 - Between 40 - 100 metres long (131 - 328 feet)
2 - Between 15 - 20 metres long (49 - 66 feet) for Sardine fishing. Over 40 metres (131 feet) ocean-going

Plate 55: Sambuk on a Pearling expedition

Plate 56: Boom under sail

Plate 57: Shua'i transporting fish-traps

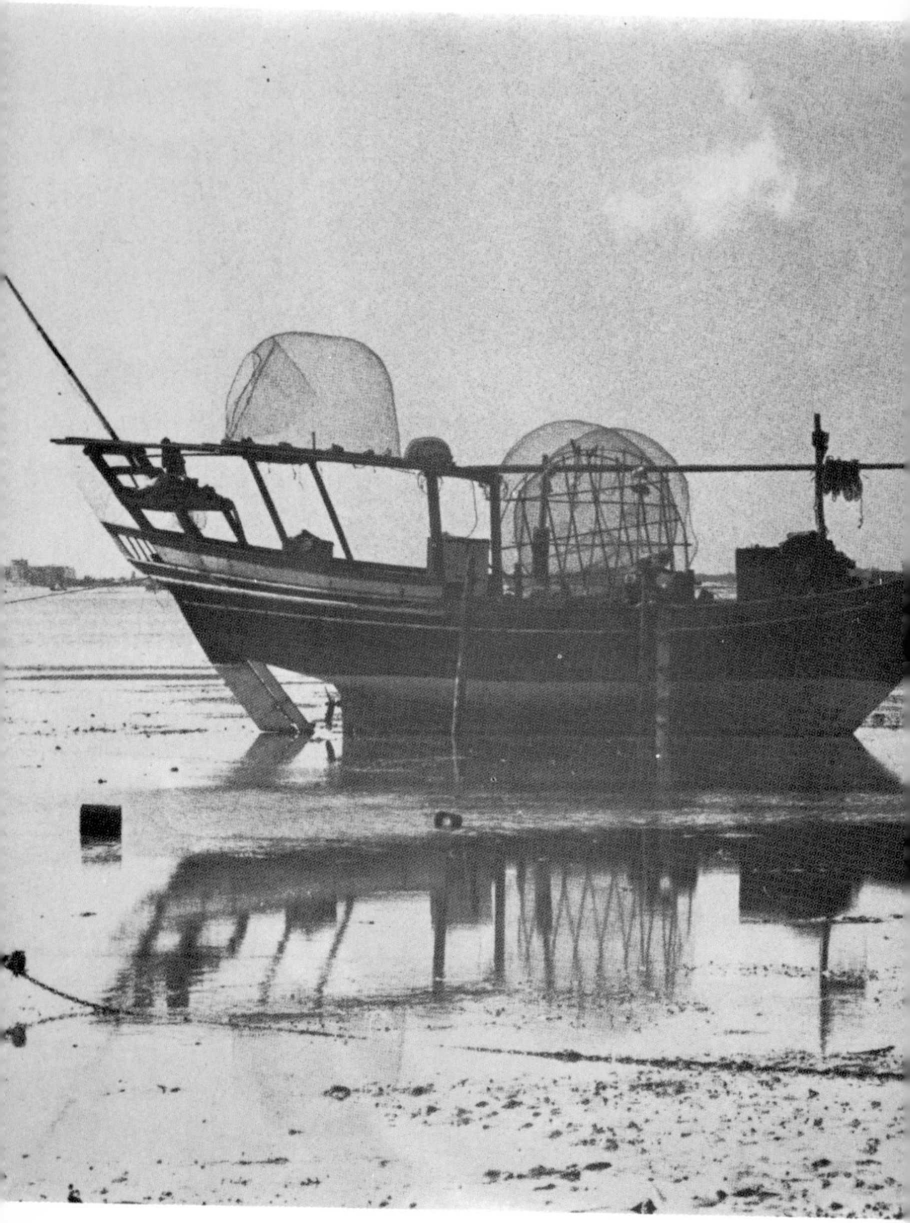

Plate 58: Bow of a Jalibut

111

Plate 59:
Dhow Building

Plate 60: Sewn sections of a dhow

The wood used for the construction of the hulls is imported from India, usually teak and mangrove. The ribs are often made from acacia which is grown locally. Traditionally no nails were used and so in the sewn construction (see Plate 60), the planks were drilled along the edge at five to seven centimetre intervals, about two and a half centimetres from the edge. Small grooves were then cut between the holes and the edge of the plank which were then butted against the adjacent plank and sewn in place. The joint was covered inside the hull with pads of palm leaves and held in place by the stitching. The ribs were inserted after the hull was completed.

The modern boats are usually made with nails, but the principle of joining the planks is similar to the old tradition of laying the planks edge to edge and adding the ribs later. Templates are used to support and shape the hull planking before the ribs are fitted, but otherwise the tools are a simple hammer, saw, adze, bow-drill, chisel, plane and caulking iron. In Route 8 you will see the dhow-builders at work where many of the old techniques are preserved. However, one or two of the craftsmen are now using power-drills to make their work less arduous.

Nail holes are drilled for each nail and a larger diameter shallow hole is cut so that the nail-head is countersunk, each nail being wrapped in oiled fibre before being driven home. The hull is caulked with palm fibre or raw cotton mixed with coconut or simsin oil. An outer coating of oil boiled with whitewash (lime) is added below the waterline, whilst the hull above the waterline is varnished.

Plate 61: Baiting a fish-trap

FISH TRAPS take two forms in Bahrain. One type looks like a large lobster pot and is constructed with **wire**. It is filled with ground bait to entice the fish through a narrow funnel. These are made at a workshop adjacent to the dhow-builders' yards (Route 8) where long coils of wire can be seen stacked up outside a shed alongside completed pots. Fishermen transport the traps to the appropriate fishing grounds by dhow (see Plate 57).

The second type is of a much more complicated nature and construction. They are **wooden traps (hadra)** which look like giant arrow-heads when seen from an aircraft. The fish trap sites are registered because of their obvious value, although unlike date-palm plantations they are not tightly controlled by the Ruling family since fish have no capital value. According to a survey made in 1934, there were 868 hadra scattered around the shores of the northern half of Bahrain island. Many have been abandoned or destroyed as a result of land reclamation for the airport, the expansion of Mina Sulman and the construction of the ASRY dry-dock and access causeway. However, examples are evident along Route 2 at Halat As-Sulatah and off the Muharraq coast near the airport, as well as beside the Sitra Causeway (Route 4). Like palm groves, fish traps are given proper names at the time of their construction. The names do not change even though the traps may be modified or sold.

Their function is to exploit the movement of the fish with the tide. During high tide the fish move towards the shore searching for food; during low tide they rush back into the deep water. The distance between the shore and the deep water, the tidal land, is highly variable and in some places is as much as eight kilometres. On their way back to the deep water, the fish are caught between the two wings (matam) of the trap and gradually move with the tide along the hand (yad) to the deepwater dip (qadil) where they are caught (Fig. 14). The trap is made of rows of palm reeds implanted in the seabed, the lower part, the qadil, being wrapped with barbed wire to prevent the escape of small fish. The hand and wings reach far into the shallow water, and the qadil extends to the deepwater line, never exceeding sixty to ninety centimetres deep in low tide.

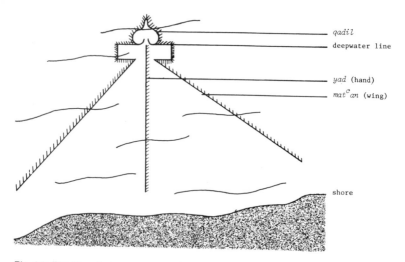

Fig. 14: Fish Trap design

From:
F. I. Khuri
Trade & State in Bahrain, page 54
The University of Chicago Press/Chicago & London

Traps are built by specialized fishermen called rassamin who may take one or two weeks to complete one trap. Hadra are not uniform in size, length, depth, the area they cover, or the type of fish for which they are designed. Different species of fish have different swimming habits and therefore require different traps.

Fishermen usually collect the catch twice a day during low tide, occasionally using donkey-pulled carts. Like palm groves, fish traps are owned by private holders who rent them to fishermen on an annual basis. The rent is always paid in cash, unlike that levied on date groves which may be paid in kind.

COFFEE POT MAKING is a dying craft in Bahrain. Although this guide does not include a visit to craftsmen manufacturing these vessels, it is worth mentioning their tradition. Bent wrote in 1889:

"The coffee pots of Bahrain are quite a speciality also coming from Al Hasa which appears to be the centre of art in this part of Arabia. With their long beak-like spouts and concentric circles with patterns, these coffee pots are a distinct feature. In the bazaars of Manama and Muharraq, coffee vendors sit at every corner with some large pots of similar shape simmering in the embers. In the lid are introduced stones to make a noise and attract the attention of the passerby".

Throughout the Arabian peninsula the basic style is the same, fashioned in either copper or silver. Local variations are introduced by craftsmen who stamp each of their wares in a similar way to the practice of gold or silver hallmarking.

EMBROIDERY is a traditional craft which still thrives in certain villages, particularly Busaibi and Sanabis. Women sew intricate designs onto their national costumes (thobe al nashel) which are sold in the Wednesday Market (Route 3). The woollen cloaks (bisht) worn by men or formal occasions are bordered with gold embroidery also.

Sir Charles Belgrave wrote some fifty years ago: "Ladies of the upper classes had their abbas edged with gold thread and decorated with big gold tassels. When the "abbas" wore out, the gold thread survived and hawkers used to go through the streets in the mornings singing 'zerri atiq, zerri atiq' (old gold thread) which they brought from the women at the house doors. They refurbished it and sold it to the makers of the abbas."

RUSH MATTING is made on Sitra island in the homes of various craftsmen. For this reason a visit is not made along Route 4. Nevertheless it is interesting to note that the material used is a grass (aseel) which is grown between the sweet spring water boundary on the land and the salt water along the sea-shore. The woven mats can be found in mosques and dwellings throughout Bahrain as well as in the permanent exhibition at the Directorate of Arts and Culture (Route 5).

Plate 62: Arabian Gulf Silver Coffee pot

HERBAL MEDICINES are a product of palm tree flowers, pollen and buds. Jidhafs village is noted particularly for this craft where one or two of the local pharmacies sell a few of these natural remedies. Visitors with both a knowledge of Arabiv and of the potions themselves, may be lucky enough to find a source of supply when driving through the village (Route 8).

LIME MANUFACTURE is carried out in the village of Aali (Route 5). Suitable stone is hewn from different parts of Bahrain, taken to the village, laid out on wood and then fired in the kilns which are adapted from the interiors of some of the burial mounds. Men with large wooden flails beat the heated stone into powder. After sieving it is used in the construction industry, mainly as whitewash.

Plate 63: Nura kilns, Aali

POTTERY is also made in Aali where traditional methods are used (Route 5). Finished pieces are dried in the sun and then taken to the same kilns which are used by the lime-makers. The jugs, water-pipes, flower-pots, and money-boxes are in daily use throughout the islands in many house-holds despite the availability of imported goods.

Recent experiments with different types of gas and oil-fired ovens may lead to a method of glazing Aali pottery which could lead to the development of an entirely new industry based on this ancient craft.

Plate 64: Aali Pottery

GYPSUM (jus) has been used traditionally in building since prehistoric times. Some of the tumuli graves were lined with the substance. It is collected from many sites in Bahrain where it is quarried in slabs from the area immediately beneath the ground surface. Frequently it is processed in situ in a similar way to lime. The resulting powder, when mixed with water, has the properties of a quick-setting cement and is used for decorative plaster-work on many house facades and interiors (see Route 1).

BASKET WORK is still practised in several villages throughout Bahrain. Hand fans and small dishes are woven in various homes in Jesra on the west coast of Bahrain. (These are not visited in this guide.) Sofra (dining mats for the floor), chicken coops and larger baskets are woven at Karbabad village (Route 8) where the weavers work under a barasti shelter in the middle of a date grove.

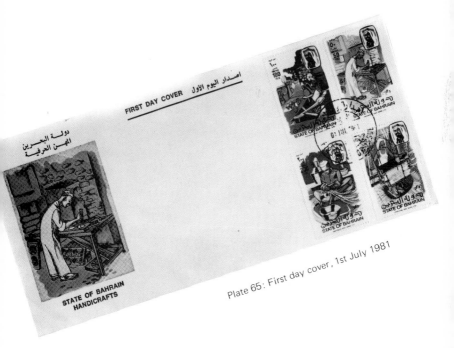

Plate 65: First day cover, 1st July 1981

Plate 66: Weaver, Bani Jamra

FABRIC WEAVING has become synonymous with the village of Bani Jamra where thirteen small centres produce a characteristic black cloth for ladies to make into a type of abbayah. Finished lengths are placed on stretchers out in the sunshine where they are covered with a starch substance and then left to dry. Visitors are welcome (Route 8) although the usual courtesy of requesting to take photographs is appreciated by the craftsmen.

Plate 67: Cloth on stretcher, drying after starching

10. ENGINEERING

WATER DISTRIBUTION SYSTEMS

As we have discussed in an earlier chapter, Bahrain's continuing importance as a trading centre has had much to do with its abundance of fresh water. Formerly, irrigation was through surface wells and natural springs, but two man-made features have facilitated a wider distribution of water to parts of the island which otherwise would not have been available for cultivation.

Plate 68: Qanat System, Dar Khulaib (Route 7)

Qanats are the older of the two systems. They are long underground water-courses or networks of tunnels, which are thought to be one of the most useful and ancient of man's creations. As they are entirely dug and not built they cannot be called structures. However, that being said, it is some considerable achievement to dig a tunnel up to 70 kilometres in length, as in the Iranian qanat system, especially bearing in mind that no mechanical equipment was used.

The name Qanat, sometimes written as Khanat, comes from the Semitic word "to dig". Current estimates put the number in use in Iran at 25,000 whilst they are also in use in Afghanistan, Egypt, Chile, Mexico and Oman. Nineveh, the ancient site in Iraq, is known to have been supplied with water from such systems.

The building of a qanat is a dangerous business, as Fig. 15 suggests. The Iranians referred to them as "the murderers". Initially, a surveyor selected a likely area for sinking a test well, based on his premise that the groundlevel vegetation suggested the presence of water not far below the surface. The test well was then dug to the impervious layer, the most frequent siting being the slope of a hillside. Since Bahrain is virtually flat and the water table high, it is possible that the conduits were dug here as open ditches, then roofed with faroush (coral conglomerate) and finally covered with earth. Certainly by studying the system near Saar village (Route 8), it is possible to look down the ventilation shaft to the floor of the channel just a metre or so below.

Fig. 15

Building a qanat: 1. Test well; 2. Ventilation shaft being sunk; 3. Working in tunnel, with windlass hauling buckets; 4. Tile hoops of drain sections being lowered to line conduct.

The test well having proved successful, a series of vertical shafts were then dug at intervals of about 40 metres, the upper few metres of which (or in some cases their entire depth) were then lined with reinforcing stones. The width of the conduit was usually a metre or so wide, and the height about half as much again.

As the conduit was dug, the excavated material was hauled up the ventilation shaft in buckets and deposited around the mouth giving it a typical crater appearance. Fig. 15 demonstrates that the principal hazard was the moment at which the tunnel was connected to the water source. If the test well had not been emptied previously, or tapped cautiously, the resultant flood would have drowned the tunnellers.

On completion, the ventilation shafts were capped with a chimney arrangement of stonework, thus enabling their periodic inspection and cleaning.

In Bahrain, it is thought that the Qanats pre-date the Islamic period, for a reference to a 7th century battle near Diraz village in which use was made of underground channels would appear to refer to them. There are two principal systems in Bahrain, although most of the channels have fallen into disuse and are either dry or in a ruinous state.

Those readers with particular interest in these structures should refer to Routes 7 and 8, although it might be helpful to mention at this point that the more extensive system indicated in Route 7 is by far the more derelict and hazardous and the least accessible. It is also likely that some of its length will be destroyed completely by a proposed new town and the Saudi Arabia-Bahrain Causeway. However, that being said, those who have access to a four-wheel drive vehicle and have the patience to walk some considerable distance will find, at the time of writing, the remnants of this ancient system.

The section mentioned in Route 8, although very short and therefore the least rewarding upon investigation, does have the advantage of being located beside a tarmac road. As such, it offers the visitor with little spare time the opportunity to grasp the qanat concept with comparatively little effort.

Artesian Wells in the 1920s and 30s Major Frank Holmes drilled many artesian wells which were to alter Bahrain's irrigation system quite radically. Jidda Island, for instance, had "no fresh water and just a solitary palm, until an artesian well was sunk which turned out to be a gusher with a head of water over 12 feet (3.75 metres) high and of better quality than the water in Manama".[1]

The introduction of artesian wells to Bahrain did much to increase the area of land which could be cultivated, but it also proved to be a mixed blessing, for in the following years so many wells had been drilled that the water table fell substantially, causing some of the islands' gardens to dry up. A sombre example of this is evident on the Shaikh Sulman Highway (Route 5), where a dying palm-grove presents a stark horizon. The island of Nabih Salih (Route 4) has suffered a similar fate in certain areas, where the water-table has fallen considerably.

The term artesian takes its name from the basin of Artois in France, where a series of sedimentary rocks are disposed in a particular way. An aquifer (a water-bearing bed of strata) holds the water under a pressure head between two layers of impermeable strata (Fig. 16). As in similar basins throughout the world, when a well is sunk into the aquifer, water rises to the surface by virtue of the pressure head and may in fact rise as a fountain if unconfined.

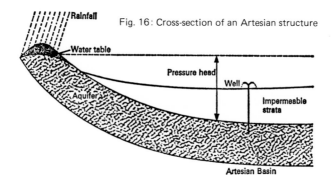

Fig. 16: Cross-section of an Artesian structure

Rainfall

Water table

Pressure head

Well

Aquifer

Impermeable strata

Artesian Basin

1 - Belgrave, C. - Personal Column

Plate 69: Windtower (Route 5)

AIR COOLING SYSTEMS

Nowadays, the electricity-powered air-conditioner has replaced the wind-tower and the wind-catcher in Arabian countries. In some ways this is a pity, since the former in particular was a distinctive architectural feature which was both functional and decorative. Climate was the determining factor in their incidence. As man could not dominate nature, he had to learn to adapt to it. The parts of the Moslem world where wind-towers and wind-catchers were built fell within the hot-dry and hot-humid tropics exposed either to land winds, which are light, dry and hot; or to sea breezes which are humid and strong.

WIND-TOWERS were designed to catch the breeze and funnel it into the spaces below. The route of the wind fell for most of its length into an enclosed cavity, and as it passed through this passage, it lost much of its heat to the surrounding walls and increased in velocity. This created air movement which then reduced the temperature in the house interior. The application of this principle varies from one location to another throughout the Middle East: the wind openings of Qatar; the wind catchers of Iraq and Iran; the Cairo type and the multi-dimensional wind-towers of the Arabian Gulf, notably Dubai and Bahrain.

Despite the fact that they require no running costs and only minimal maintenance, wind-towers have declined in importance in recent years and many of them have fallen into disuse. However, several are still visible in Bahrain, particularly in the conservation area of Al-Awadiyah (Route 5).

A wind-tower operates according to the time of day and the presence or absence of wind (see drawing page 130). The walls and airflow passages of the towers (2) absorb heat during the day and release it to the cool air at night. The next day the walls are cool. When there is no wind, hot ambient air (solid arrows) enters the tower through the openings in the sides (1) and is cooled when it comes in contact with the tower. Since the cooler air is denser than the warmer air, it sinks down through the tower, creating a downdraft (2, 3, 5,). When there is a wind, the air is cooled more effectively and flows faster. Doors in the lower part of the tower (4, 6) open into the central hall and basement. When these doors are open, the cooled air from the tower is pushed through the building and out of the doors and windows. When there is no wind at night (broken arrows), the tower operates like a chimney. Warm air rises, creating an updraft.

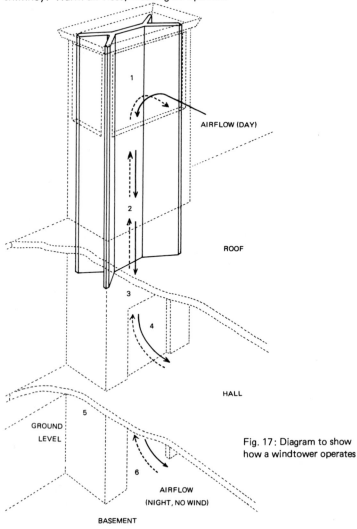

AIRFLOW (DAY)

ROOF

HALL

GROUND LEVEL

AIRFLOW (NIGHT, NO WIND)

BASEMENT

Fig. 17: Diagram to show how a windtower operates

Wind-Catchers (Badgirs) are common in two forms in Bahrain: mid-wall wind-catchers inside rooms and roof-top parapet wind-catchers.

Mid-wall wind-catchers are usually built in upper rooms, where they catch wind movement across the single-storey roof-tops. They are particularly favoured for use in the reception room (majlis), but are also known in other rooms. There are good examples in nearly all the houses already conserved or proposed for conservation.

Roof-top parapet wind-catchers are designed to deflect wind down on people sleeping on the roof-tops on hot summer nights. Most of the old houses in Bahrain were built with them.

It should be noted that the mid-wall and parapet wind-catchers are almost entirely restricted to Bahrain and are one of the most characteristic and distinctive features of the islands' architecture. Early in the 20th century they seem to have appeared for the first time in Dubai, and subsequently in Kuwait, in both cases apparently under Bahraini influence.

Fig. 70: Wind-catchers in the upper register of a house (group of three arches at sub-roof level)

Arad Fort

Gudaibiya Palace

PART III: LOCATION GUIDE

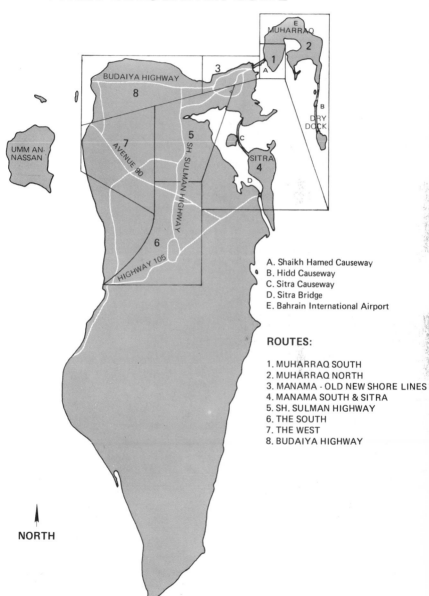

A. Shaikh Hamed Causeway
B. Hidd Causeway
C. Sitra Causeway
D. Sitra Bridge
E. Bahrain International Airport

ROUTES:

1. MUHARRAQ SOUTH
2. MUHARRAQ NORTH
3. MANAMA - OLD NEW SHORE LINES
4. MANAMA SOUTH & SITRA
5. SH. SULMAN HIGHWAY
6. THE SOUTH
7. THE WEST
8. BUDAIYA HIGHWAY

NORTH

ROUTE 1 - MUHARRAQ SOUTH

1 SH. ISA'S HOUSE
2 MOSQUE
3 SIYADI HOUSE
4 SH. SALMAN'S HOUSE

NORTH

MUHARRAQ SOUTH

ROUTE 1 - MUHARRAQ SOUTH

Until the 1930s Muharraq was the centre of political power and economic prosperity in Bahrain. The Al-Khalifa family and many of their supporters lived in what had been formerly a walled town, divided into fifteen quarters named after Arab tribes or segments of them.

Several factors have combined to reduce Muharraq's importance politically, economically, and demographically: namely the decline of the pearl industry in the mid-thirties; the relocation of the Ruler's residence to Manama, Sakhir and later Rifaa; the construction of the oil refinery; the gradual growth of Manama to become the islands' commercial and administrative centre and creation of a new urban centre, Isa Town.

Fortunately, these events have changed the visual structure of Muharraq town comparatively little. It is still characterised by narrow streets typical of an Arab town, retaining many of the features which were built at the height of what has been regarded as one of Bahrain's main periods of architectural enhancement, the nineteenth century.

In 1869 A.D. when Shaikh Isa bin Ali Al-Khalifa was summoned from exile in Qatar by the British to be declared Ruler of Bahrain, he brought a period of calm and political stability to the islands. Although he did not order the building of the house which was his home for many years, he did order the construction of many buildings in Muharraq and Manama.

Shaikh Isa's contempories were well aware of this architectural impetus. Shaikh Khalifa ibn Ahmad al-Habhan travelling from Mecca wrote: "the first thing that engages the eye in Bahrain is the splendid arrangement and position of the palaces of the nobles. The palace of His Excellency the Ruler (Shaikh Isa) stands in the middle, while all around are the palaces of his noble sons, so that it seems to be moon among the stars. To the south is the palace of his son, His Excellency Shaikh Hamad (east of Jami Mosque); to the west is the palace of His Excellency Shaikh Abdullah, to the north is the palace of his son His Excellency Shaikh Muhammad and to the east the palace of his grandson Shaikh Khalifa bin Salman; all other palaces of the family surrounding it on all sides just as the halo surrounds the moon or the covering surrounds the fruit; and all of them are fine and elegant and geometrically pro- portionate."1

The aim of Route 1 is to recapture the essence of Shaikh Khalifa's observations.

It is worth noting that the three houses which we shall visit are protected by keepers and, whilst access is normally gran- ted upon request, it is unlikely to be permitted near to midday and afternoon prayer times. For your comfort and conve- nience it would be advisable to arrange your visits to finish before 11.45 a.m. or to start after 3.30 p.m., so that lunch- time and the heat of the day can be avoided also.

The starting point may be reached by leaving the Hilton/ Sheraton Hotels (facing the sea), turning to the right along King Faisal Highway, and proceeding to the set of traffic lights at the intersection of the Shaikh Hamed Causeway. The Diplomat Hotel is on the right.

Turn left to cross the Causeway. This was opened in 1942 with the completion of a steel *Swing Bridge* designed to allow dhows under sail to pass along the deep-water channel twice a day into Muharraq harbour (Mina Muharraq). As the volume of road traffic increased and diesel engines replaced wind-power at sea, the toll-gate was discontinued and the swing-bridge became obsolete. Today, an elevated 4-lane road-bridge replaces the swing-bridge although plans ann- ounced in 1981 indicate that this will be widened shortly to accommodate six lanes of traffic.

After driving along the Causeway for a few hundred metres it is possible to see *Abu Mahur Fort* on the south shore of Muharraq by looking to the right. This is where the Ruler, Shaikh Abdulla, was besieged in 1843. As tugs may obscure the view and it is inadvisable to park on the Causeway, a quieter opportunity to see the fort is provided in Route 4.

Cross the bridge, pass through two sets of traffic lights at 1.5 kms. and 1.7 kms. (that is, from the Diplomat Hotel traffic

1 - Chronicle of Al-Khalifa - English Translation.

View from Sh. Hamed Causeway across to Abu Mahur Fort.

lights). Move into the right-hand lane so that a 2.0 kms. you may turn right at the roundabout into Shaikh Abdulla Avenue, distinguished by a water-tank on the right.

One hundred metres after the turn a small open space is located on the right. Should you wish to take a diversion to the Suq it is suggested that you park your vehicle here since the lanes leading to the market are particularly narrow and often congested. Road 1125 located fifty metres beyond the parking space (indicated by a no-entry road sign) and Road 1123, a further 5 metres ahead, both lead into the heart of the Suq.

When mobile once more proceed along Shaikh Abdulla Avenue, up an incline and into a small square, (2.3 kms.). It is at this point that Route 1 really begins since it is the edge of the main conservation and restoration area of the important palaces and houses of Muharraq.

The first palace which we shall visit is Shaikh Isa's House (Bait Shaikh Isa), which can be located by continuing until the kilometre gauge reads 2.5 kms. Turn left into Road 916. At this point the west wall of Shaikh Isa's Palace will be on your right. Select a convenient parking place and walk to the main entrance in the north elevation of the Palace.

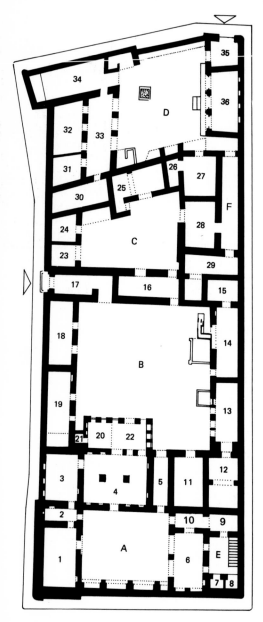

Fig. 18

SHAIKH ISA'S HOUSE -
Key to Ground Plan

A - Shaikh Isa's Private Court

B - Women's Court

C - Servants' Court

D - Men's and Visitors' Court

E - Small Court

F - Open-Air Passage

Ground-Floor Rooms

1 - Shaikh's Apartments

2 - Hammam

3 - Children's Room

4 - Family Majlis

5 - Passage

6 - Portico

7 - Hammam

8 - Hammam

9 - Store-room

10 - Passage

11 - Store-room for date-honey

12 - Servants' living quarters

13 - Portico

14 - Coffee preparation room

15 - Store-room for timber
and palm fronds

16 - Bread-kitchen

17 - Main Entrance

18 - Women's majlis

19 - Shaikh's daughter's
apartment

20 - Entrance to family majlis

21 - Open cupboard

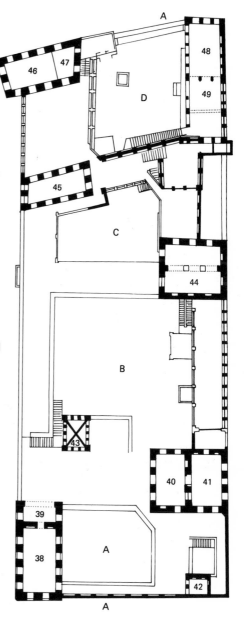

22 - Entrance to family majlis
23 - Laundry
24 - Kitchen
25 - Hammam
26 - Small, windowless room
27 - Business majlis
28 - Kitchen
29 - Cow-shed
30 - Living quarters or kitchen
31 - Hammam
32 - Men's living quarters
33 - Portico
34 - Men's living quarters
35 - Entrance
36 - Portico
37 - Passage

Fig. 19
KEY TO FIRST FLOOR PLAN

38 - Children's living quarters
39 - Entrance liwan
40 - Portico
41 - Shaikh's apartments
42 - Store-room
43 - Windtower
44 - Apartments of married
     son and wife
45 - Apartments of unmarried
     women of household
46 - Visitor's apartments
47 - Hammam
48 - Majlis
49 - Covered terrace •

139

THE HOUSE OF SHAIKH ISA (Bait Shaikh Isa) was built in the 19th century by Hasan ibn Abd Allah ibn Ahmad al-Fatih, on the estate of Shaikh Abd Allah.

For many years it was the residence of Shaikh Isa bin Ali Al-Khalifa, the present Amir's great-grandfather, and was not abandoned until 1972. Since that time it has become dilapidated through neglect and would have been destroyed totally to create space for a public square had it not been for the intervention of Shaikha Haya Al-Khalifa, Director of Archaeology and Museums. The house was bought later by the Department of Antiquities and restorations were undertaken in 1976 with a view to transforming it into an Ethnographic Museum. However the task is immense as any visitor will observe and as investigators discovered in November 1977 when an expedition from the French Archaeological Mission entered the house for the first time. It requires not only time and money for restoration, but also a commitment to preserving traditional techniques and skills which cannot be replaced by 20th century technology and speed. This is particularly true of the decorative carving, which is being re-created painstakingly by one of the few remaining gypsum carvers living in Bahrain.

It will be several years before the work is complete, even to the point of structural safety. In this respect visitors should take special care when wandering around the first floor terraces. Fractures in the staircases, cracks in the floor, and a lack of protective balustrading create hazards for the unwary and for unaccompanied children. For this reason, as well as for the preservation of the restored sections, a guard is stationed by the main gateway in road 916, although access is normally available. Should the doors be closed, a persuasive knock will usually summon the custodian to help you.

Women's Court (B) - Ground Floor

On entering the main gateway and dihliz or vestibule (17 on the ground plan) turn right (and west) into the largest of the four Courts (B). This is the Women's Court and by tradition of Moslem society, it communicates directly with the exterior and not with the Servants' Court (C) or the Men's and Visitors' Court (D). Access to these latter two courts from the interior of the house on the ground floor elevation, is only by way of the bread-kitchen (Room 16).

Originally Court B was based on a square plan of 18 metres per side, but room additions (20 and 22), a cupboard (21), and a windtower added by Sh. Isa's wife Aisha, have since modified the plan.

Opening off the northern facade of Court B are two rooms, each with their own entrance. One of them, Room 19, served as the private living quarters for the Shaikh's daughter, and the other, Room 18, as the women's Majlis (reception). It is interesting to note that subsequently this room was altered to become an apartment for Shaikha Haya Al-Khalifa's grandmother.

Modern additions (a staircase and a workman's shed) have obscured the southern facade of four arches. By way of two of these arches one enters Room 13, a liwan (portico) where the ladies would sit and embroider during the hot weather. The other two arches open into a room (14) where coffee was prepared. The site of the tannur (fireplace) can still be seen. To the rear, on its eastern side is a store-room (15) for wood and palm fronds. Moving west, an area (20/22) juts out and half conceals this elevation. It appears as a type of wide portico or entrance to the family Majlis, above which rises the wind-tower. A flight of stairs leading onto the first floor is set between the wind-tower and wall on the northern facade.

Adjacent to the Majlis entrance is a polylobed arch which serves as an opening to a covered passage (5) leading to Court A, the Shaikh's private Court. It is in this covered passage that the visitor may see intricate gypsum carvings in the walls, as well as evidence of the gypsum carver's current restoration work.

To the south of this passage is a rectangular door that leads to a store-room for dates (11) in which date-honey (al-mudabbasa) was made.

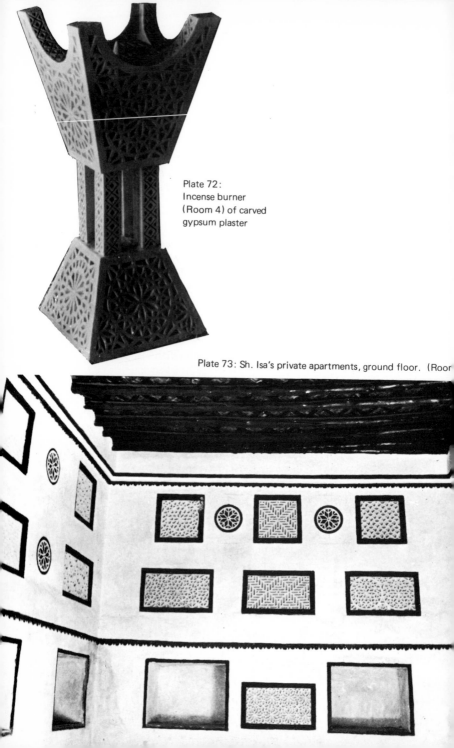

Plate 72:
Incense burner
(Room 4) of carved
gypsum plaster

Plate 73: Sh. Isa's private apartments, ground floor. (Room

Sh. Isa's Private Court (A) - Ground Floor

Passing through the covered passage (5), one enters the Shaikh's Private Court. To the north are his private apartments (1) and his hammam (2) (bathroom). On the eastern side of the main court (A) a door leads onto a spacious, hypostyle hall, used as a family Majlis (4). On the south side of the court is the liwan (portico) where Shaikh Isa died in 1932 A.D. (1351 A.H.). To the east of the liwan is a small passage (10) which leads to a small inner courtyard (E), adjacent to which are a hammam and latrines (7 & 8). From this small courtyard, a staircase (at present in an unstable condition) leads onto the first floor.

Plate 74: Passageway entrance (5) beside the date-honey store (11) beneath Sh. Isa's first floor apartments (41)

Plate 75:
Portico entrance to Sh. Isa's
first floor private apartments (40).

Sh. Isa's Private Court and the Women's Court - First Floor

By taking the staircase just mentioned up to the first floor, a small windowless room at an intermediary level on the southern face will be noted. This was for the laying-by of weapons.

On reaching the top of the staircase, Sh. Isa's apartments (41) and a portico where tea was served (40) are on the right. To the left of the staircase is a small store-room (42). By walking across the terrace, the visitor comes to rooms 38 and 39. (These are directly above the Shaikh's ground-floor private apartments and hammam (1 & 2). The majlis which we have just entered is an impressive room enclosed by ten shuttered windows, which even in the heat of the summer, is surprisingly cool. This room was used as the children's living quarters during the summer, replacing room 3 on the ground floor.

By walking across the parapet from the children's quarters, one is above the ground floor rooms 18 and 19. The upper part of the wind-tower (43) is level with the terrace, consisting of a register of four blank trefoiled arches along its length, and three across its breadth. A corresponding number of narrow bays open out over the first register. The crenellation on the tower was put in place during restoration work.

Servants' Court (C) - First Floor

By continuing along the northern terrace, we face the west wall of room 45. Turning to the right and then to the left, a view of the ground-floor of Courts C and D presents itself. Architecturally, room 45 is arranged in such a way that it belongs as much to Court C as it does to Court D (the Men's and Visitors' Court). However, Claire Hardy-Guilbert suggests in her monograph, "La Maison de Shaykh Isa a Bahrayn" that "the fact that this room was meant to house the unmarried women of the household obliges one to consider it as belonging to Court C, even to the Women's Court (B), via the terraces. It is trapezoidal in plan and contains ten windows, two of which look onto the street. They have wooden shutters and it is very probable that originally there were no windows on the eastern facade (facing the men's building)."

"On the south side of the terrace is room 44, which gives onto the street (now named Shaikh Abdulla Avenue) via two bays, each of which is composed of geminated arches, the lower part of which is partially closed by rectangular stucco gratings. Another bay, on the northern face, has the same kind of opening".

From this terrace we may descend either by way of a staircase above Court C, or retrace our steps back to the staircase leading from Court A. It will depend much on the safety of the staircases themselves and the current state of restoration work as to which is the more appropriate.

Servants' Court (C) - Ground Floor

This is narrower than the previous two courts and has comparatively fewer rooms. Those on the north side, Rooms 23 and 24 were the laundry and kitchen. Another kitchen to the south gives way to an open-air passage (F) to communicate with a blank-walled stable to the west and the men's court (D) to the east by means of a passageway (37).

Men's and Family Guest Court (D) - Ground Floor

This is located at the east end of the palace and like Court B has its own entrance from the street outside. The two main rooms are 36 and 32 on the plan. At the time of writing both were in the process of restoration. A portico is situated to their south (33), its upper part being outlined by a frieze of semi-circles placed side by side. A dimly lit room to the east (34) has been restored and demonstrates the type of multicolour decoration described in chapter 8. The soffits of the beams have been painted and the matting roof construction is clearly visible. Under the west staircase you will find the entrance door to a small business majlis (27) where visitors could meet the Shaikh's servants.

Men's and Family Guest Court (D) - First Floor

There are four main rooms on this level. A guest room (46) surmounted by a masonry balustrade with a frieze of triangular merlons is located on the north facade with an adjacent hammam (47). A similar arrangement occurs on the south side of the house, where room 48 provided guest accommodation, preceded by a porch (49).

Mlle Hardy-Guilbert suggests that, whilst this house may not be the best example of a 19th century Bahrain residence, it is the most representative of the large houses in the Muharraq district. It is for this reason that we have indulged at this location more than otherwise might be the case in a guide of this nature.

Upon leaving Shaikh Isa's House, turn right. Upon reaching the corner of the house, look to the left where you will see a *fine facade of a private house* as well as an impressive example of a carved wooden door. To the right at the far end of the east facade of Shaikh Isa's House you will note another carved doorway with a gypsum plaster archway. Although the door is locked, it leads into the ground floor of the Men's and Visitors' Court, (35 on the ground floor plan).

Retrace your route to Road 916, turn right into Road 911, left along Road 913, at which point the mud-brick minaret of an old mosque will face you (Plate 76). Behind this you will observe the carved gypsum plaster exterior of Siyadi House. On approaching the mosque turn right into a small square. Follow Lane 914 which forms a passage between the east facade of Siyadi House and adjacent buildings.

Turn left down Lane 910. The main entrance to the house can be distinguished by an imposing wooden doorway on the left bearing an unusual canopy. Once again, should the door be closed, a knock will usually summon the guard to assist you.

SIYADI HOUSE is one of the most impressive houses open to the public. It is noted in particular for its magnificent majlis. Formerly it was the home of a pearl merchant, evidence of which is supplied in the form of a substantial safe built into a corner of an upstairs room.

The house has been renovated extensively by the Department of Antiquities and displays many of the decorative and ornamental features mentioned in chapter 8. In particular the ceilings should be noted in the ground floor rooms. It is unfortunate that at the time of writing much of the floor area

Plate 76: Mosque adjacent to Siyadi House.

has been disturbed as rising salts and damp have damaged the restored walls. The same problem was experienced in Shaikh Isa's House during the restoration process.

The ground floor contains an ante-chamber for visitors which is located to the right of the entrance. A fine ceiling with brightly painted beams should be noted. Kitchen quarters are located on the left of the entrance passageway behind which is a courtyard. The far end of the entrance vestibule opens out onto a small central courtyard to the left of which is an arched majlis where another safe was found. The doors should be noted for their carved decoration.

The arrangement of the rooms is designed to accommodate seasonal changes. Immediately above the small ground floor majlis is a room with a few windows facing the courtyard. This would have been used in the winter.

On the terrace level, reached by either of the staircases leading from the central courtyard, a light airy room designed for use during hot weather can be distinguished by a small carved wooden door with a centre post and latch (Plate 52, chapter 8).

The terrace provides a good position from which to view the exterior of the majlis which is dominated by the chequer-board effect of carved gypsum plaster recesses in various designs. Access may be gained by either of the doors in the west facade. It should be noted that one of these may be secured from the inside in order to prevent a through-draft should both doors be opened at once. Upon entering either of the lower rooms of the majlis, the reason for this caution will become obvious.

The larger of the two rooms is panelled with window shutters around the four walls, above which are semicircular frames containing panels of stained glass (Plate 77). The right wall upon entry is the partition to the smaller lower majlis. By opening one of the wall casement it is possible to go through into the second room which is distinguished by mirrored shutters (Plate 78). The door for this room opens out onto the terrace, beside which you will see a safe built into the wall. Either of the exterior doors will provide

Plate 77: Main majlis, Siyadi House

access to all sections of the majlis. The reason for limiting this to one door only is to prevent the wind blowing the frames of the shutters and smashing the stained glass and mirrored panels. Should you open them to obtain a better view or to take photographs, please take care to secure them afterwards.

The main majlis is dominated by the middle and upper registers of carved plaster panels as well as an ornate ceiling. The window shutters which are on the right wall adjacent to the exterior terrace window lead onto a spiral staircase. The women's room is at the top from where an excellent view of the main majlis can be gained. Extreme care should be taken when looking through the upper chamber window as it is on a narrow ledge at the top of the narrow spiral staircase. There are no protective balustrades.

Plate 78: Smaller room of main majlis, featuring mirrored shutters.

Chapters 7 and 8 provide a more detailed description of the architectural construction features and the traditional forms of decoration.

After visiting this house, retrace your steps to your vehicle in Road 916. Turn left into Shaikh Abdulla Avenue, then one hundred metres later, turn right at the traffic lights into Shaikh Isa Avenue. 300 metres ahead on the left hand side you will see the facade of Shaikh Salman's House. If parking space allows, pull into the left of the street, before the no-entry sign ahead, and leave your car outside the Shaikh Salman Health Centre. If this is not possible, turn right into Shaikh Hamad Avenue, then left 50 metres later into Road 1349, left again 100 metres beyond into Road 1301 and left again into Shaikh Isa Avenue a further 100 metres ahead. In other words, drive round the block so that you are facing the point where it was suggested that you park your vehicle beside the Health Centre. Having made this diversion, you will note a square on your right, where parking space is usually available.

SHAIKH SALMAN'S HOUSE (BAIT SHAIKH SALMAN)

This is one of the oldest residences in Muharraq, built and lived in by members of the Al-Khalifa family during the nineteenth century, and then used sporadically as a guest house until it was abandoned in 1973.

It has been allowed to fall into disrepair, but nevertheless it still demonstrates many outstanding features, representative of the period in which it was constructed. Particularly note-worthy are the carvings in the upper floors and one of the doorways in the lower court. At the time of writing the house was undergoing extensive renovation. However the guard, on being assured that one's interest is genuine, will normally allow access to the premises, and may even show visitors round to ensure that the more hazardous parts of the house are avoided.

Having completed this route, retrace your way back to Manama. Should you wish to continue your tour of Muharraq, turn to Route 2, which begins at the "water-tank" round-about at the begining of Shaikh Abdulla Avenue, marked on the map.

ROUTE 2 - MUHARRAQ NORTH AND EAST

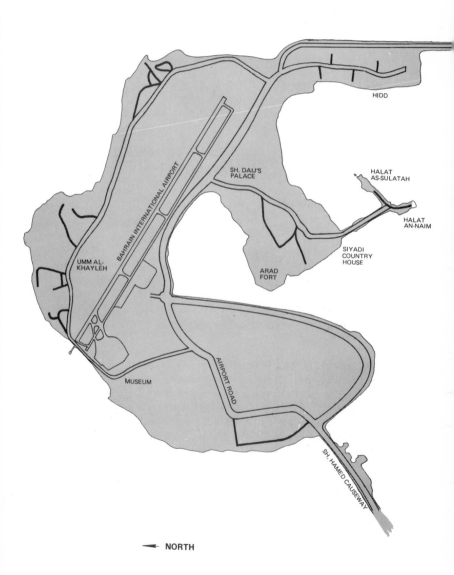

HIDD

SH. DAIJ'S
PALACE

HALAT
AS-SULATAH

HALAT
AN-NAIM

BAHRAIN INTERNATIONAL AIRPORT

SIYADI
COUNTRY
HOUSE

UMM AL-
KHAYLEH

ARAD
FORT

AIRPORT ROAD

MUSEUM

SH. HAMED CAUSEWAY

NORTH

ROUTE 2 - MUHARRAQ NORTH AND EAST

To join this route from Manama, start at the Hilton/Sheraton Hotels, face the sea, turn right at the traffic lights along King Faisal Highway, and proceed to the traffic lights at the intersection of the Shaikh Hamed Causeway. The Diplomat Hotel is on the right.

Turn left across the Causeway, cross the bridge, pass through two sets of traffic lights until you reach the first roundabout (2 kms. from the Diplomat Hotel). This is distinguished by a water-tower on the opposite side of the intersection, with Shaikh Abdulla Avenue being indicated on the right and Shaikh Sulman Avenue ahead.

Those joining this route from the end of Route 1 should take this as their starting point. For the convenience of everyone, this roundabout will serve as a zero-point for the following kilometre readings.

Proceed to the 3rd set of traffic lights from this landmark, the first being at 1.1 kms., the second at 1.6 kms, and the third at 1.9 kms. A fire-station and petrol-filling station are on the left of this junction. Turn left into Avenue 20, follow the road for just over a kilometre (cumulative reading 3.1 kms.), and turn left into Road 2601 signposted on the fence to the National Museum. Turn right, left and immediately right again into the forecourt of the Museum (3.3 kms.).

THE BAHRAIN MUSEUM is housed in the former Officers' Mess of the British Royal Air Force base in Bahrain. When the RAF left in 1967 the premises were converted to house a fine collection of exhibits in two galleries representing the ethnography and archaeology of the islands of Bahrain. The Museum is open from 07.00 - 13.00 every day, excluding Fridays and Public Holidays.

Many of the artefacts which have been excavated from burial mounds and settlements during the last century are displayed in the Archaeology Gallery. Particularly worthy of note are the pottery and tumuli displays, the stamp seals and statuary subjects. The Ethnography Gallery contains a decorative display of national costume, various crafts, armour and a series of cases illustrating the pearl diving traditions. Elsewhere there is a small display of documents, mainly in the Arabic language.

Upon leaving the museum, turn left at the gateway into Road 2605 and proceed to Avenue 20, remembering to zero your kilometre gauge upon your departure. Turn left and follow the airport perimeter road which will take you along the northern extremity of Muharraq island and of the Bahrain islands as a whole. It is possible to see reed fish traps (hadra) of the type described in chapter 9 along the coast.

Plate 79: City V (Qalaat Al-Bahrain)
artefacts on display at the National Museum.

Plate 80: Mrs. Edward Skinner, together with a member of the Yateem family,
standing beside a Hannibal aircraft, early 1930s (other gentleman unidentified)
Note the long "Spade" being used to turn the propeller blade.

Plate 81: Bahrain Airport, Muharraq, early 1930s.

BAHRAIN INTERNATIONAL AIRPORT has seen many changes during its half century of existence. In the early 1930s the first building was a simple barasti arrangement (Plate 81), beside which there was a sign which read:
"4 bells - aircraft about to approach
2 bells - signal to embark
6 bells - aircraft will depart

In 1932 the first Imperial Airways aircraft landed in Manama. However it was not until take-off that it was discovered the ground beneath its wheels concealed a disused water channel, whereupon the machine sank and had to be dug out of its predicament. Since that time, the airport has been developed in various stages on the present site in Muharraq.

A new building was opened in 1961, followed by a terminal specifically designed for jumbo jets and other wide-bodied aircraft in 1971. No account of developments at Bahrain International Airport would be complete without mention of the Concorde aircraft. When Flight BA 300 touched down in Bahrain on 21st January 1976, the islands' airport achieved a special place in aviation history by becoming the first airport in the world to announce the arrival of a scheduled supersonic passenger flight. The last Concorde flight to leave Bahrain was in November 1980.

Passenger through-put is now over three million a year with a forecast of 5.7 million by 1995. In order to accommodate this expansion a new departure terminal is being built as part of the first phase of a 15 year master plan to develop the airport still further.

At 3.6 kms. from the Museum you will pass a dairy project on the right. This farm is the site of the *Umm Al-Khayleh spring*. On the north coast of Muharraq the former palaces of Shaikh Isa the first were located at Rayyan and Samahidj. Unfortunately, they have since been demolished.

Three hundred metres further along the road you will note a second dairy project set back from the road on the left. Follow the airport perimeter road, until it meets with Hidd Avenue, (spelt Haidd on the sign) at 6.6 kms. Turn right, and then left at the traffic lights (8.0 kms). Adjacent to this

Plate 83:
Halat An-Naim
Mosque interior.

junction is a somewhat derelict building which is now used as a workers' dormitory. It was built about half a century ago as a *summer palace for Shaikh Daij bin Hamed*, one of former Ruler Shaikh Hamed's sons.

Follow the Arad Road for 900 metres. Bear left at the next junction which is marked by a water-tank on the left and a Fish Shop sign on the right. Continue straight ahead, passing glades of palm-trees and aseel grass (used for rush mat weaving) until you come to an intersection in the middle of a village at 9.6 kms. Facing you, nailed to a pole, is a sign reading Road 4213. Turn left into what is Avenue 28. (Having made the ninety degree turn you will then see the Avenue 28 sign on the left hand wall). Proceed for a few metres, bear right, then left, following Avenue 28 until the palm-glades open out to the sea. Immediately before the school on the right hand side is a date-palm garden.

THE SIYADI FAMILY'S COUNTRY HOUSE, located in the garden, can be seen from the road where the vegetation is not too dense. Although the house is largely ruined, it is worth a visit to look at the fine examples of gypsum carving exposed on the walls of the upper majlis and the women's balcony at the rear. The general layout of the house is a two-storeyed design built around the central courtyard set in a pleasant setting of trees with a supply of running water. The best approach is via the garden entrance. Follow the track round the house, but care should be taken as the building is becoming more derelict.

Beyond the school at 10.2 kms. a narrow causeway road begins as the link to the islets of Halat An-Naim and Halat As-Sulatah. These are dormitory communities with pearl diving traditions.

HALAT AN-NAIM MOSQUE is on the right after you have negotiated the first stretch of the causeway (11.0 kms.) At the time of writing a new housing community was being constructed around the perimeter of the islet which is to incorporate the restored mosque. The original minaret has been demolished (see Plate 43) and a new one built into the new section of the building plan. The restored sections focus on the wooden decoration on the panelling around the facade and a type of crenellation around the edges of the flat roof. Its foundation is thought to have been about one hundred years ago. The mimbar (pulpit or speaking-place) is incorporated into a recess which designates the direction of Mecca. Plate 83 demonstrates the ornamentation of this feature.

By taking the second leg of the causeway to *Halat As-Sulatah* you will have the opportunity to see the reed fish-traps staked into the shore on the right hand side past the bus-stop (11.6 kms.) If the tide is low, the outline as described in chapter 9 will be much clearer.

Another former dormitory community for pearl divers is situated at *Hidd*, on the opposite side of the bay. Nowadays, this has developed into a small town, providing homes for many residents who make the daily journey into Manama for employment.

Retrace your route to the centre of the village and the road intersection of Avenue 28 and Road 4213 (2 kms. from Halat As-Sulatah.) Turn left and proceed for one hundred metres. (Although the signs are a little confusing, you are in fact travelling along Road 4213.)

Plate 84: Fish traps on the shore of Halat As-Sulatah. Hidd is on the opposite shore.

At the next junction the road bears right to become Road 4231, whilst Road 4213 continues straight. Keep your course and do not turn. Proceed past the village buildings at the end of which you can check your position by locating another Road sign 4213 on the right-wall. From this bearing the village gives way to agricultural developments on each side of the lane which narrows quite considerably. 700 metres beyond, it will come as a surprise to find yourself driving onto the beach. Upon turning right you will face Arad Fort.

ARAD FORT

Recent archaeological excavation by Shaikha Haya Al-Khalifa and Dr. Monik Kervran have shown that this was not originally an Omani fort as was once thought, but that the later phase was built on the inner walls of a Portuguese fort of a most elaborate kind, with dual concentric surrounding walls and corner bastions separated by a space which contained buildings. In this form it is shown in the early Portuguese maps of Bahrain, such as that in the Bibliotheque Nationale de Paris. The presence of an original outer moat was also established.

The fort possesses two distinct problems which will become apparent when looking at the structure. The first is the conservation of the deteriorating bastions, which are liable to collapse within the next few years, unless they can be supported from further sea and sand erosion. The second problem is the need to excavate the moat and outer walls, in order to learn more of the original Portuguese occupation level, without disturbing the structural stability of the Omani installation above them.

Studies so far have concluded that the fort was built during the brief Omani occupation around 1800 and its whole appearance suggests a rapidly constructed fortification with the emphasis on defence rather than decoration. Its position is a strategic one between Muharraq peninsula and Muharraq town as well as overlooking the straits which provide a channel to Bahrain island. A depression in the central courtyard indicates the presence of a well or spring. In places it is possible to see the walkway, or look-out platform, around the upper part of the walls, protected by what was originally a crenellated wall. Large beams were built into the walls for greater strength and at the time of writing were still visible. The only attempt at decoration is the "pre-cast" plaster curve over the inner side of the entrance. The purpose of the roof holes in the entrance arch is unclear.

Upon leaving Arad Fort, retrace your route to the traffic signals on the main road (adjacent to Shaikh Daij bin Hamed's summer palace). Turn left and continue towards the International Airport. Take the last exit at the roundabout (2.1 kms. from the traffic lights). As you travel along the coast road, Arad Fort will appear on the left at 4.0 kms. Five hundred metres beyond at the next set of traffic lights there is another opportunity (other than in Route 8) to see a dhow building operation.

The *Coastguard Base* is on the left a kilometre beyond. (For those taking an excursion by boat to the Howar Islands to investigate the flints as mentioned in chapter 5, it is advisable to inform the coastguards of your destination and estimated time of return.) This new complex conceals the remains of *Abu Mahur Fort* (Route 4). It is worth asking the guard at the gate if you might visit the fort, although access cannot be guaranteed. At 6.7 kms. Route 2 ends with the traffic signals at the end of Shaikh Hamed Causeway. Turn left to Manama.

Plate 85: Arad Fort.

ROUTE 3 - MANAMA - OLD AND NEW SHORELINES

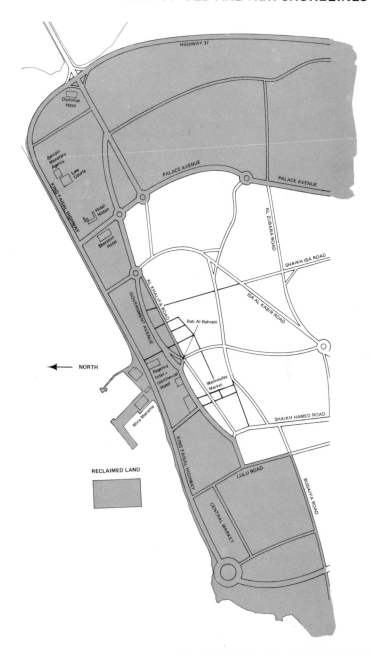

ROUTE 3 - MANAMA - OLD AND NEW SHORE-LINES

MANAMA (meaning the sleeping place) is the capital and the largest town of the Bahrain islands, situated in the northern low-lying part of the main island. Although known to have existed in the sixteenth century, Manama has no ancient buildings dating from that time. In the last quarter-century, an extensive programme of land reclamation has taken place to the north and east of the town, followed by a vast programme of highway construction and office development. Change has occurred so swiftly that even the young generation of residents in Bahrain will remember some of the changes which have taken place along the shore-line in less than a decade. It is therefore the intention of this route to take the reader along the line of the old shore prior to land reclamation, and then along the present coast road as it appears in 1981.

For the convenience of those readers unfamiliar with Bahrain, we will start from the *Hilton and Sheraton Hotels*. With your back to the sea and the Sheraton Hotel on the right down Government Avenue, pause to look across the dual-carriageway to a small mosque which nestles between the Paradise Restuarant and a new office block on the right.

The mosque is known locally at *Masjid Ras Rummaan*, literally meaning Mosque of the Headland of Pomegranates. As the name suggests, the minaret of the old mud brick style, one of the few remaining examples in Manama, stands on a former headland behind which groves of pomegranates used to be grown. Your present observation point was the sea until thirty years ago, as was the reclaimed land to the left of "Paradise" Roundabout.

Continuing down Government Avenue towards the next roundabout, you pass the *British Embassy*, on the left, with the British Council to its right. A photograph in the Embassy archives taken in the early 1940s shows the sea lapping against the boundary wall.

Leave the roundabout at the 3rd exit and turn into Al-Khalifa Road. This is land-marked by the "Wimpey" Cafeteria and a palm-tree on the right hand corner. Park your vehicle at a convenient place before proceeding down Al-Khalifa Road. Walk to the central reservation of Isa Al-Kabir Road. (This would have been the 4th exit from the roundabout had you not turned into Al-Khalifa Road).

From this position you will see a walled garden to your left, behind which there is a school. This is the site of the **Adviserate**, the home of the late Sir Charles and Lady Belgrave. Ahead is the **Manama Centre,** with **Government House** situated nearest to the roundabout, distinguished by a "honey-comb" style of sun-baffle around the building's exterior. By comparing Plates 86 and 87 you will see that the horizon of fifty years ago presents a somewhat different picture from that of today.

Immediately on the left down Al-Khalifa Road, you will see examples of **mud-house architecture**, **wooden balconies**, **doorways** and **stained glass windows**, typical of the type mentioned in chapters 7 and 8.

Return to your vehicle and continue along Al-Khalifa Road. After 100 metres you will reach the **Friday Mosque** on the corner of Road 525. This has been mentioned already in chapter 4 as one of the indispensable features of Moslem urban life. It was built by Shaikh Hamed in 1938 with the revenues from the first oil sales. A particularly interesting feature is the minaret decorated with colourful mosaics in varied geometric designs.

The Almoayyed Buildings are located on the right at 0.25 kilometres - Road 403 is opposite. These twin structures built by Yusuf Almoayyed in 1956 on the site of his grandfather's timberyard, were the first high-rise buildings to appear in Bahrain. Opposite is Almoayyed Stationery, a shop sited where Mr. Almoayyed recalls he used to moor his boat when he was a boy.

A few metres beyond this shop on the right side of Al-Khalifa Road is a china and glass store, Al-Mahmood Stores. This was built on the site of the first premises of the **National Bank of Bahrain** which celebrated its silver jubilee in 1981. The present seventeen-storey headquarters of the bank now towers behind

Plate 86: 1981 - Sh. Isa Al-Kabir Road,
looking towards Bahrain Tower (left),
Manama Centre (middle)
and Government House (right).

Plate 87: 1930s - Sh. Isa Al-Kabir Road
from the same vantage as Plate 86.
The Adviserate garden is on the left.
Note the sea ahead

Plate 88: Bait Skinner, Al-Khalifa Road, early 1930s. (Now Jashanmal's department store)

on reclaimed land, adjacent to the modern Government Avenue and parallel to Al-Khalifa Road.

Opposite the china and glass-ware shop is an office block with Awal Stationery shop on the ground floor. *Bait Skinner*, the first Manama home of Mr. and Mrs. Edward Skinner between 1932-1937, was situated on this site until it was demolished in 1956 (Plate 88). Mr. Sinner was BAPCO's first Vice President and during his five year stay in the house he used to entertain many of the visitors to Bahrain since "in those days there was only the sea-front road between the house and the sea. There were few buildings at all in that part of Manama". On one occasion he was visited by the French pearl expert, Monsieur Pack, who pointed to a cupboard in one of the rooms and explained that it had been the store place for the most valuable pearl ever landed in Bahrain. The pearl now forms part of the late Barbara Hutton's collection of gems.

When the house was demolished the site made room for the new premises of the *British Bank of the Middle East* (whose doors feature impressions of seal-stones excavated at various sites in Bahrain) and the new Jashanmal department store.

167

The Old Law Courts are opposite the Jashanmal department store. However, with the 1981 completion of the new Ministry of Justice and Islamic Affairs in the Diplomatic Area, this 1937 building will be vacated shortly in preparation for its conversion into a Museum of Culture.

Turn left at the far corner of the Jashanmal building (0.4 kms), pass the Habitat store on the left, turn right at the end of the street (0.5 kms.) into Abu Hurairah Avenue, and as you proceed forward, a modern mosque appears on your left and Hussain Yateem's impressive glass-faced shopping centre on your right. When Mr. Yateem ordered the construction of this building, he made only one proviso - it must be built around *the three trees* which used to stand on the water's edge when he was a boy. He recalls, "I used to sit under them, sometimes fishing, sometimes dreaming. There was a Scottish woman living in the house that stood just here. I remember how she loved to wake each morning to the sunlight streaming through her window and listen to the sound of prayer from the mosque on the corner. She taught me to love and respect the trees, and when she and her husband moved to Australia, I remained and so did the trees".

Plate 89: Panorama as seen from Manama Centre

At the far corner of the Yateem Centre (0.6 kms) Al Muthanna Avenue faces you. By turning to the left you will find yourself on the edge of the Manama Suq, a lively emporium of shops where the cloth and gold suqs in particular are worth a visit (refer to the map relating to this Route). However, for the purposes of our story, we will not digress from the shore-line. Instead we will turn right beside the Yateem Centre and head for the Al-Khalifa Road intersection where the Bahrain International Communications building is located on the right corner and the Rafidain Bank on the left. Proceed straight ahead to the end of Al Muthanna Avenue where it meets Government Avenue. There we find ourselves standing on the old shore-line of the 1950s.

Plates 89 & 90 legend:

1 British Bank of the Middle East
2 Jashanmals Department Store
3 Old Law Courts
4 Yateem Centre
5 Bahrain International Communications
6 Bahrain Maritime & Mercantile International
7 Former long-distance dhow harbour now Government Avenue
8 National Bank of Bahrain car park
9 Citibank Building
10 Unitag House
11 Chartered Bank
12 Bab Al-Bahrain roundabout
13 Former Customs Pier
14 1938 Petrol Filling Station

Plate 90: Continuation of Plate 89 with overlap.

Turn ninety degrees to the right, *The Bahrain Maritime and Mercantile International building* (formerly Gray Mackenzie) is on the right. It was just in front of this that the long-distance dhows used to tie up (see Plate 91). The area which is now occupied by the National Bank of Bahrain and the Chamber of Commerce (see Plate 93) was the sea. Please note that the 1950s view is not reversed by accident. The change to right-hand driving did not take place until 17th November 1967. However even this panorama will change when Bahrain's first multi-storey car park has been constructed in front of the National Bank of Bahrain.

Plate 91: Dhow harbour prior to land reclamation.
Bahrain Maritime and Mercantile building, background.

Turn to face the sea and the *Port of Manama (Mina Manama)* Customs Offices. In front of them is a set of traffic lights which mark the approximate end of the former pier, originally mounted with several cannon recalling the days of raids and attacks on the islands (see Plate 92).

Plate 92: Cannon on the old pier, now King Faisal Highway.

Plate 93: Government Avenue, 1950s, sea to the left.
Now the National Bank of Bahrain site.

Plate 94: Bahrain's first petrol-filling station opening ceremony, 1938.

Plate 95: Bab Al-Bahrain, built 1945. Note carved gypsum balustrade (now demolished.)

Turn left again. The *Regency Intercontinental Hotel* and car-park are in the foreground. You will have completed your circle of vision when you see a *petrol station* which was in active service until early 1981 (see Plate 94). At the time of its opening in 1938, it was the first petrol station in Bahrain and what is thought to have been the first in the lower Arabian Gulf. As the story goes, the builders had no idea what a petrol station should look like and so it was designed in the classic proportions of a mosque, hence the very high roof and arch-way design.

If you are walking, now turn left down Government Avenue. If you are in a vehicle, turn right past the Bahrain Maritime and Mercantile International Building mentioned earlier, pro-ceed to the top of Government Avenue, go round the "Wimpey" roundabout and retrace your route down the opposite side of the road until you are level with the petrol station once more. Less than a hundred metres beyond you will see a little roundabout with a wide archway to the left.

This is called *Bab Al-Bahrain (Gateway of Bahrain)* and was designed by Sir Charles Belgrave in 1945, to house the Govern-ment offices of the time (Plate 95). It looked out onto the *Customs Square and the Pier*, which as Sir Charles noted in his memoirs "was a fascinating, lively, noisy place where there was always something new to look at; often there were as many as a hundred dhows anchored off the pier and tied up alongside. One saw many types of seamen from the Gulf ports and from more distant places. There were stocky, dark men from Sur, below Muscat, wearing ochre-coloured clothes, yellow headcloths or red skull caps; lean, long-haired Muscatis with hawklike features, often accompanied by one or two lascivious youths; Persians, wearing tall felt hats loose, full-sleeved robes, with wide woolen shawls round their waists and Indians from the Malabar coast who came ashore from their big sailing ships, which were usually the largest in the port. Their ships' sterns were elaborately carved and had rows of windows with brightly painted shutters. Often the Indians brought with them little green parrots in cages to sell to the Arabs. Longboats, full of men who sang as they rowed, moved between the dhows and the pierhead, and coolies shouted and sang as they shouldered heavy sacks, loading and unloading cargo oт every conceivable kind."

Plate 96: Old Customs Pier and Harbour, 1930s (Compare Plate 90).

Plate 97: Government Avenue, 1950s.
Looking towards Bab Al-Bahrain.
Mr. Jashanmal's old store is on the left.

174

"Citibank" building and *Unitag House,* both modern office complexes are diagonally opposite the Bab Al-Bahrain. Fifty years ago, this site was part of the harbour scene which has just been described. By the mid-1950s the area had been reclaimed and Mr. Jashanmal had built his first store on it (Plate 97). Zero your kilometre gauge.

We now follow the old shore-line down Government Avenue past the new *Chartered Bank*, also built on reclaimed land and opened in June 1981, (0.2 kms from the petrol station). At 0.3 kms is a left hand turning, distinguished by the Bank Melli Iran sign displayed prominently on the Shaikh Mubarak Building on the corner of the street. It is this road which leads to the *Wednesday market*, referred to in chapter 4.

Continue past the Delmon Hotel (0.4 kms.) to where the building density begins to thin out on the right hand side to reveal undeveloped reclaimed land. Just beyond this point (0.6 kms) you will see Bahrain's first "picture" (movie) house which was constructed in 1937, the *Pearl Cinema.*

As we turn right at the junction just after the Tylos Hotel (0.8 kms) and head towards the bus station and the new *Central Market* (1.1 kms), we have completed our tour of the old shoreline. The market is worth a visit if only to see the colourful displays of fruit, vegetables and spices.

By contrast, the second part of the route takes us along the new King Faisal Highway where development is still in progress. At the time of writing the following buildings of interest have been completed or are under construction. With the Central Market on your left, turn right into King Faisal Highway at 1.4 kms (the reading continuing from where we zeroed after the petrol station diversion).

Mina Manama, where the long-distance dhows now come into port, is on the left at 2.0 kms; on the right is the newly completed Regency Intercontinental Hotel. Travel past the traffic lights, located on the site of the *old pier*. The *Chamber of Commerce Building* is on the right (2.4 kms), followed by the *Manama Centre* (2.6 kms) and *Government House* (2.7 kms). The current construction work in front of this building is the new *Ministry of Finance and Foreign Affairs*, scheduled for completion in 1982.

175

Plate 98: Mina Manama, 1981

The **Sheraton Hotel** complex is beyond the next road intersection (3.0 kms.) followed by a set of traffic lights at 3.3
kilometres. (By taking the right hand fork immediately
prior to the lights you will return to where our route started.)
On this corner, the new headquarters of the **Gulf International
Bank** are under construction.

The open space beyond the traffic lights presents a panoramic
view of the prestigious **Diplomatic Area**. The recently-
completed **Ministry of Justice and Islamic Affairs** (distinguished by its fort-like appearance) and the **Bahrain Monetary
Agency** (bearing facsimiles of the Dilmun seals) are dominant
landmarks among the numerous adjacent office blocks (3.5
kms).

Continue along the Highway. The **Kuwait Embassy** and the
Holiday Inn are on the right at 4 kilometres. The **Diplomat
Hotel** is on the right 500 metres later, prior to the Shaikh
Hamed Causeway junction. It is at this point that Route 3
ends.

For those wishing to return to the Sheraton and Hilton Hotels,
fork right before the traffic lights down the slip-road to the
Diplomat Hotel and Central Manama. Bear right at the second
turning, taking the Alhasan Building as your land-mark on the
right corner.

Plate 99: Diplomatic Area, 1981 Ministry of Justice and Islamic Affairs (right); Bahrain Monetary Agency (left).

Before continuing down Road 1708 ahead, pause to look left across the central reservation of the dual carriageway you have just turned off.

Bait Al-Koran (House of the Koran) is to be built on the site which at the time of writing is vacant. This "minaret for Islamic and humanitarian thought" will form an international centre. It will comprise a mosque, a library containing over 40,000 Islamic books, a museum with five exhibition halls for the display of important Koranic works and calligraphy, a school for the teaching and the recital of the Koran and a lecture hall for conferences and meetings.

Dr. Adul Latif Kanoo, the Bahrain Historical and Archaeological Society's President, is the driving force behind this unique Islamic centre, the foundation stone of which will be laid on 16th December 1981, Bahrain's National Day.

Proceed to the roundabout ahead (5.5 kms) adjacent to the Route 3 starting point.

Plate 100: Model of Bait Al-Koran

ROUTE 4 - MANAMA SOUTH AND SITRA

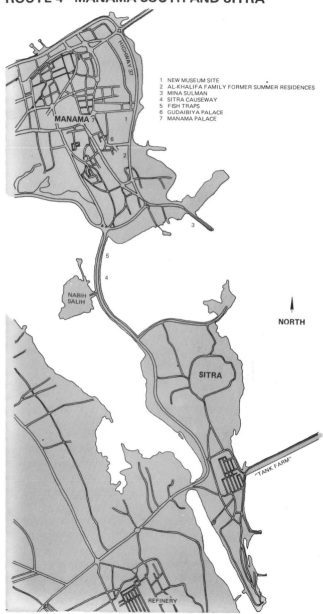

1 NEW MUSEUM SITE
2 AL-KHALIFA FAMILY FORMER SUMMER RESIDENCES
3 MINA SULMAN
4 SITRA CAUSEWAY
5 FISH TRAPS
6 GUDAIBIYA PALACE
7 MANAMA PALACE

ROUTE 4 - MANAMA SOUTH AND SITRA

The starting point for this route is the Hilton/Sheraton Hotel forecourt. Facing the sea, turn right at the traffic lights along the King Faisal Highway. Continue to the intersection of Shaikh Hamed Causeway where the traffic lights indicate the beginning of Highway 37 ahead.

Proceed from this junction for 0.8 kms., at which point to the left you will see the **Fort of Abu Mahur**, across the bay. A map in the Bibliotheque Nationale de Paris almost certainly depicts this military installation protecting the island of Muharraq at the time of the Portuguese occupation in the sixteenth century. The Fort was rebuilt in its present form in 1840 by Shaikh Abdulla Al-Khalifa, who was to be besieged there three years later by his great-nephew Muhammad bin Khalifa bin Sulman Al-Khalifa, until he surrendered to go into exile in 1843.

Only one of the four original bastions still stands, the remaining three having been razed to the ground during the turbulent years of the nineteenth century. At the beginning of the twentiety century it was used as a quarantine station, after which it was allowed to fall into considerable despair. Recently the Department of Antiquities has restored its remains, with the intention of building low walls projecting just above ground level to enable visitors to see the full extent of the original ground plan. (However, it should be noted that access from the land side (Route 2) is through the new Coast Guard Base and that a visit to the Fort cannot be guaranteed upon request.)

At 2.4 kms. further along Highway 37, a large open space presents itself on the right. This is the site of a new **Civic and Arts Centre**, which will include new premises for the National Museum at present housed in the former RAF Officers' Mess building at the now disused Muharraq Air Base (Route 2). It is hoped that the project, now in the planning stage, will be complete in 5 years.

The rear elevation of the **Guest Palace or Gudaibiya Palace** (2.7 kms.) forms the backdrop of this site. It is worth commenting that ten years ago the palace garden wall was adjacent to the sea-shore.

The next set of traffic lights (2.9 kms.) serves as a preliminary landmark to the next point of interest. The new Gulf Hotel complex is on the right. The gold dome of the Juffair Sports' Stadium is on the left. Locally it is known as the *Juffair Sports Dome*.

Highway 37 intercepts a group of the *Al-Khalifa family nineteenth century summer residences* (3.5 kms.). Those to the right have fallen into disrepair, the courtyard of one now being used as a store. However, by looking over a section of the collapsed wall it is possible to grasp the concept of the layout and distinctive architectural features. An interesting carved wooden door is still evident at the rear.

Plate 101: Al-Khalifa family nineteenth century summer residence.

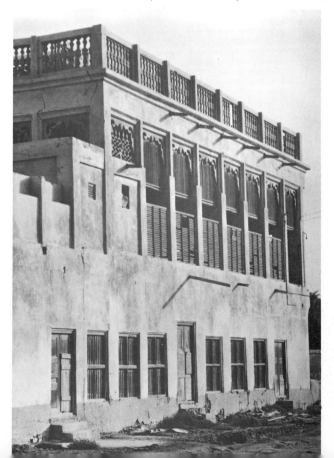

Plate 102: Part of the Al-Khalifa family's nineteenth century summer residence, courtyard.

Pass through the next set of traffic lights (3.9 kms.), bear right at 4.6 kms., at which point, the port gates of **Mina Sulman** are located on the left. Bahrain's deep-water container terminal, named after the late Ruler (the present Amir's father), was opened in 1967.

Continue ahead taking note to move into the left hand lane at approximately 5.7 kms. ready to turn left into Highway 31, the beginning of the **Sitra Causeway**.

At the time of writing, this intersection is distinguished by a set of traffic lights and evidence of the highway terminating abruptly just a few metres beyond. During the next four years a fly-over will be built over the junction and the area ahead reclaimed from the sea to facilitate the completion of the eastern extremity of the Bahrain-Saudi Arabia Causeway.

The Sitra-Manama Causeway, completed in 1977, forms an essential link to the island of Nabih Salih (apparent to the right), and the industrial complexes which have been established on the island of Sitra. If it is low tide as you pass along the Causeway, you may be fortunate to see exposed fish-traps on the far left at 6.6 kms. (of the type described in chapter 9). However, it will be far easier to recognise their features on the return journey, even if the tide is high, since the central reservation will not restrict your line of vision.

The bridge to **Nabih Salih** is indicated at 7.7 kms. It is worth a diversion to drive through the palm-glades, some of which unfortunately have died due to a lowered water-table. Well into the twentieth century pilgrims travelled by boat to pay their respects to the tomb of the Saint, after whom the island is named, and to bathe in the fresh-water springs of Ain Ar-Raha and Ain Al-Mahazza.

The Nabih Salih village life-style is a reflection of a rural community's limited exposure to modern western society. The women and children dress in colourful fabrics and wander about the lanes with considerable abandon, whilst the males congregate to discuss the way of the world making little concession to traffic thoroughfares. It is therefore advisable to exercise caution when driving round the island and to respect Moslem traditions by not taking photographs, especially of the women who may feel apprehensive of visitors.

Plate 103: Sitra "Tank Farm"

Upon leaving the island by the bridge, turn right towards the island of **Sitra**. Just less than two kilometres ahead the causeway ends to join the island itself. At 3.2 kilometres further along the route the petroleum company's storage **"Tank Farm"** spreads out to the left for some considerable distance. For those who wish to visit the perimeter of the Refinery, follow the indicating sign at the roundabout 3 kilometres beyond. This is more or less where Sitra bridge used to link the island to Bahrain island. (If you did not digress to Nabih Salih island, the reading on your gauge as from the beginning of the route should read 15.7 kms. at the roundabout.)

Return to Manama retracing your route as far as the traffic lights on Highway 37 at the Gulf Hotel. The Juffair Sports Dome will be on your right. Turn left to pass the hotel, also on the left. Cross the intersection ahead. The Ramada Hotel is on the left and a large garden with a fountain on the right forms a foreground to the **Gudaibiya Palace** used to host foreign heads of state and important visiting dignitaries.

Proceed to the next roundabout. On the left you will see the **Manama Palace** complex which was built for the late Ruler Shaikh Hamed and was later lived in by his son, Shaikh Sulman. In 1968 the Al-Khalifa family moved to take up residence in West Rifaa. Subsequently the palace was converted into a teachers' training college which continued to function until 1978. Since its closure the premises have remained empty.

Leave the roundabout by the second exit down what used to be called Old Palace Road and is now renamed Palace Avenue. After 750 metres, having passed through one set of traffic lights, you will approach another roundabout to the left of which you will see a **mosque** which is particularly worth noting.

A **multi-dimensional windtower** of the type described in chapter 10 is visible quite clearly down the street adjacent to the mosque and on the opposite side of the roundabout.

By taking the second exit from the roundabout and continuing down Palace Avenue past Ashraf's department store you will approach the Hilton/Sheraton Hotels' starting point for Route 4.

Plate 104: Gudaibiya Palace, 1981

Plate 105: Manama Palace, c. 1940.

ROUTE 5 - SHAIKH SULMAN HIGHWAY

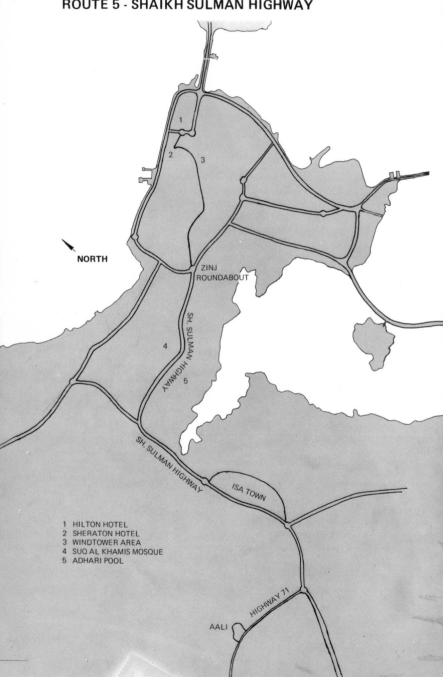

NORTH

ZINJ
ROUNDABOUT

SH. SULMAN HIGHWAY

SH. SULMAN HIGHWAY

ISA TOWN

1 HILTON HOTEL
2 SHERATON HOTEL
3 WINDTOWER AREA
4 SUQ AL KHAMIS MOSQUE
5 ADHARI POOL

HIGHWAY 71

AALI

ROUTE 5 - SHAIKH SULMAN HIGHWAY

In order to reach the Shaikh Sulman Highway and the main portion of this route, it is necessary to travel some distance through the centre of Manama. In so doing, we shall look at some of the places of interest which we pass before reaching the Shaikh Sulman Highway itself.

Commencing at the Sheraton and Hilton Hotels, with your back to the sea, turn right at the facing roundabout down Government Avenue. Take the 4th exit at the following roundabout down *Isa Al-Kabir Road*. The British Council building will appear immediately on your left after the turning.

Proceed down this road for 0.3 kms. At the junction of Road 649 on the left, you will note the Ibn Sinna Health Centre. This turning will serve as a landmark on our return, so that we may visit the *Al-Awadiyah conservation area* where the *wind-towers* (referred to in chapter 10) are situated. However, since the main purpose of this Route is to travel south, the visitor may either make this diversion a separate excursion, or bear in mind that if this location is selected for the first visit, ample time should be allowed to complete the rest of this tour, (see preceding map).

Continue along the Isa Al-Kabir Road, past the *Family Bookshop* and *American Mission Hospital* on the left (0.8 kms.) to the set of traffic lights (0.9 kms.). Immediately past this intersection you will see a traditional *ga'wa*, on the right. This is a meeting place for the local male population where they come to drink tea or coffee and smoke the *gidu* (waterpipes) from midday until well into the late evening hours. Next door is an *Arab Bakery*. By pulling into the turning just past the shop on the right, you may pause to watch the baker work the flat unlevened dough. As he tosses the loaves onto the inner wall of the clay oven, it is interesting to note the orientation of the opening facing the baker.

When we reach Aali village further along this route, we shall see these ovens being made at the pottery, where it is less easy to identify their function since during construction they are built like a bell, with the opening which we have just noted appearing as a hole at the top. In other words, when the ovens are placed in situ for use, the "bell" is turned ninety degrees with the base secured against a wall or flat surface. The qidu are also made at Aali.

On the other side of the next roundabout (1.6 kms.) stand two large gateways reminiscent of a fortress. These are the entrances to what is now the headquarters of Bahrain's Public Security Forces and therefore it is not possible to visit the compound. However, the complex is worthy of mention since it is indeed the site of a fort, *Qalaat Al-Diwan*, built in the first half of the 18th century in the reign of Nadir Shah. Originally it consisted of four round towers joined by crenellated walls. Sometimes referred to as Manama Fort or the Police Fort, it is also reputed to have been the summer residence of Shaikh Isa bin Ali Al-Khalifa during the nineteenth century. Fifty years ago, the mounted section of the Police Force was stationed at the Fort.

Leave the roundabout by the second exit, at which point the Isa Al-Kabir Road becomes Shaikh Mohammed Avenue (1.7 kms.). Continue to the 2nd set of traffic lights (2.3 kms.) after which we join the northern sector of Shaikh Sulman Highway. At 2.7 kms. pass the *Water Gardens* on the right, just prior to reaching a roundabout (3 kms.). This is sometimes referred to as the Zinj Roundabout (after the district's name) or the Dilman Roundabout (after a garage of that name on the opposite side).

For the benefit of those who join Route 5 from a different direction, (see map) this landmark serves as a secondary starting point. Those who joined the route at the Hilton/Sheraton Hotels should zero their kilometre gauge once more.

At 2.4 kms. you will approach the imposing twin minarets of the *Suq Al-Khamis Mosque*. Local tradition has it that the mosque was built by the Umayyad Caliph Umar bin Abdul Aziz in 692 A.D., but an inscription found on the site and since built into the doorway of the western minaret, suggests a foundation date during the second half of the 11th century, attributing its construction to Abu Sinan Mohammed bin al-Fadhl Abdulla. It is known that the mosque was rebuilt twice, initially it is believed about 1340 A.D., and again in the

15th century. It is during this latter phase that the twin minarets were constructed.

Apparently, the first structure was a small mosque with timber columns supporting carved timber beams. Three of the original beams are displayed in the Bahrain Museum. All of the pillars have now disappeared, although two of them used to be exhibited in the old museum until 1965.

The second phase of rebuilding seems to have been the addition of a number of rows of masonry piers, comprising squat single or double columns carrying simple pointed arches. According to a recent UNESCO conservation report, it should be noted that the corners of the surrounding wall had imitation circular bastions of a type which is known only from very early mosques of the 7th to 9th centuries. Therefore the local belief that the mosque's foundation be attributed to the 7th century Caliph Umar bin Abdul Aziz may, after all, be more appropriate than the inscription indicating an 11th century first phase.

The mosque, now in ruins, was restored to some extent by the Bahraini government in 1950 and again by Iraqi technologists in 1976. In an effort to prevent further deterioration, access to the sanctuary is restricted, although a general view can be obtained by looking over the boundary wall.

Adjacent to the mosque, is the site of *the Thursday Market (Suq Al-Khamis)* which was held regularly until the 1960s (see chapter 4).

Bilad Al-Qadim, the former capital of Bahrain in the Middle Ages, was built on the habitation mounds of an earlier Islamic city. Although little remains of the town today, it is significant to note that its ruins look towards the coast on the opposite side of the Shaikh Sulman Highway from the Suq Al-Khamis Mosque. It is believed that in the 16th century, certainly at the time of the Portuguese occupation, the twin minarets served as a landmark for the ships making harbour, which prior to extensive silting was much closer inland. Nowadays it is even harder to identify the original coastline since considerable land reclamation is being carried out beyond the silted shore-line in preparation for the new

Plate 106: Suq Al-Khamis Mosque.

Bahrain-Saudi Arabia Highway link to Mina Sulman.

Taking the chosen route south from the Suq Al-Khamis Mosque, proceed for almost 2½ kms. beyond a set of traffic lights, to where you will notice expansive groves of date-palms (4.8 kms.). In some places these present a stark montage of frondless palm trunks, the result of a lowering water-table over recent years.

Continue along the Highway, passing 2 roundabouts, the 2nd of which at 8 kms. marks the northern extremity of *Isa Town*. This is a new town built for Bahraini citizens, the Amir having donated the land so that the inhabitants only have to repay the construction costs of their houses. The first stage provided homes for 15,000 people of all income groups, the eventual aim being to house 35,000. The present development beside the Highway is part of this programme. A comprehensive range of services has been incorporated into the town's design, including a large sports stadium and Olympic-size swimming pool.

At the third roundabout (9.8 kms.) turn right along Highway 71. After travelling for almost 2 kms. you will enter the village of *Aali*. Before you reach the main mosque distinguished by a large gold dome, turn right at 11.6 kms. to the pottery. This is located a few hundred metres ahead on an incline on the opposite side of a relatively open space. From this vantage point you may observe three important features of the village; the *Pottery*, the *Nura (lime) kilns*, and some of the *ancient burial mounds*.

The pottery is operated by a family of three brothers who inherited a tradition from their father. The clay for their vessels comes from Rifaa in two forms, yellow and red, the latter being the weaker of the two. In order to maintain a regular strength and consistency, 3 buckets of red clay are mixed with 11 buckets of yellow in a trough beside the pottery. When sufficient water has been added to create the necessary blend, the mixture is left for 3 days in the sun. In order to make the clay stronger, a quantity of powder is sprinkled on its surface during the evaporation process. The clay is then removed and ready for use.

Plate 107:
Plant pots.

Plate 108:
Water-pipes.

Plate 109: Money-boxes.

The pottery's most popular product is the gidu (water-pipe) many of which can be seen lying in rows on the nearby hillside. Most of the daily output of 40 is exported to Saudi Arabia. Three other popular vessels are the children's money-boxes, the incense burners and the decorative flower pots (see Plates 107, 108, 109).

Under the shade of the palm tree beside the clay-blending trough, you may see a bread-oven under construction. In the early stages all you will find is a ring of clay on the ground, just a few centimetres high. As the potter creates the "bell" which we spoke of earlier, he will build up the walls of the oven, gradually curving them inwards, until the top is reached. At this point a rim of clay is moulded around the edge which will form the opening for "firing" and baking bread.

The clay vessels are first sun-dried as demonstrated in the photograph illustrating the rows of water-pipes. They are then fired in one of the kilns situated towards the top of the slope behind the pottery, where limited space requires the products to be stacked on top of each other for this process. Since glazing necessitates each object to be separated during the firing procedure and stricter temperature control for a successful finish, the pottery does not employ this technique

Plate 110: Bread oven (right) with the foundations of a new oven (foreground). A clay-mixing trough is under the tree.

at the moment. However recent experiments with oil and gas-fired kilns suggest that it may not be long before a new technique is introduced at Aali.

Around the pottery are the remnants of what are known as the "Royal" burial mounds ascribed to the 3rd millennium B.C. Over the years many of these have been damaged or plundered and, in the case of those immediately in the vicinity of the pottery, have been utilised as kilns for the other local industry of *Nura (Lime) Manufacture*. On driving along Highway 71 towards the village you may have noticed columns of smoke rise from its centre. Now that you are facing the kilns, you may be fortunate enough to see them being stoked with wood, after which plumes of black smoke usually billow from the furnace. Nura is manufactured from a stone which is quarried from different parts of Bahrain and taken to Aali. The blocks of white rock are placed in the kilns and "fired" for 8 hours. .After the flames have died down and the fire has burnt out, water is poured onto the smouldering blocks which crack on contact and disintegrate. The fragments are beaten into a fine powder by using large wooden flails. After it has been sieved, the powder is then bagged and exported to Dammam and Al-Khobar (Saudi Arabia). Limited quantities are retained for the home market, mainly in the construction industry as whitewash.

Plate 111: "Firing" a lime kiln.

The Aali Tumuli are the tallest and most imposing of the many thousand to be found elsewhere in Bahrain. Fig. 20 shows the location of those which are situated in the environs of the village, although it will soon become apparent to the visitor that those which have not been utilised as kilns, have been fenced off to prevent further destruction. However, a good idea of their concept can be gained by walking around the site and perimeter fencing.

There are over 100,000 burial mounds in Bahrain, covering an area of approximately 32 square kms. (20 sq. miles), comprising what is believed to be the largest prehistoric cemetery in the world. Those at Aali represent a very small proportion of them. Almost all of the mounds at this site were opened and entered in antiquity, and subsequently robbed of their contents.

The tallest mound at Aali stood over 24 metres high (80 ft); 9 were over 20 metres (65 ft) and 5 others more than 15 metres (50 ft). Lying to the right of the main village road (see map) is a large mound marked P, followed by Mound C which is now half demolished. Mound X has a single-storeyed grave, the east opening being clearly visible from the road. The grave has two alcoves at each end and a niche and step in the west wall. Its walls are plastered and there are peg holes head high along each side.

Unfortunately, part of the capstone has fallen recently and at the time of writing, has partially blocked the entrance. Behind Mounds X and C, and opposite, are the largest Aali mounds. Two in this group in particular, B and E consist of double-storeyed burial chambers. (For a fuller explanation of their features, refer to chapter 5, Part II).

Scientific interest was first shown in the tombs in 1879 when Captain Durand, First Assistant Political Resident, carried out a brief survey for the Government of India. He opened one of the largest mounds (A) but found nothing but rubble in it. He was followed in 1889 by Theordore Bent and his wife who investigated Mounds B and C, and M. Jouannin, a Belgian, who opened Mound D in 1903. Major excavation was conducted by Major Prideaux in 1906, who opened tombs E, F, G, H, to the north of the road, and I, J, K, L, M, to the south.

In 1925 Ernest Mackay excavated an additional 35 tumuli in the district of Aali, a few of which were double-storeyed mounds. An impressive view of one of the main areas of tumuli can be gained by driving through Aali village towards Buri (Route 7). Upon leaving Aali retrace your route along Highway 71 to the roundabout on the Shaikh Sulman Highway. You may choose to continue south. In this event, select Route 6.

Your return to Manama is via the third exit of this roundabout, land-marked by the *Traffic Directorate Headquarters* on the right. Remembering to zero your kilometre gauge at this point, you will note *University College* one kilometre ahead on the right. Behind this are the masts of the *Television Station*, and the premises of the Ministry of Information's *Directorate of Arts and Culture*, which houses a permanent display of local handicrafts, and an exhibition of paintings by local Bahraini artists (open from 07.00 to 13.00 Saturdays to Thursdays). The *Gulf Polytechnic* is located near to the next roundabout (1.5 kms.) after which is the main *Isa Town Gateway*.

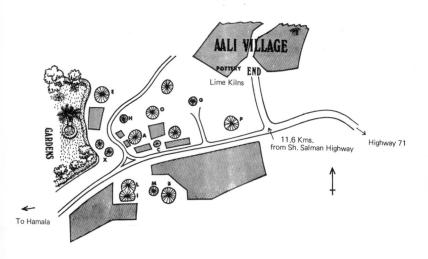

Fig. 20: Aali Village "Royal" Tumuli.

Plate 112: Windtower in the Al-Awadiyah area.

Continue towards Manama, past the next roundabout at 3.6 kms. (landmark Marhaba Supermarket on the right corner) until you reach the traffic lights (5.7 kms.).

Your next turning is 700 metres beyond the traffic lights. As it is not clearly marked, take a bearing 500 metres after the traffic signal at Alqaisi Trading, the large Honda showroom. 200 metres after this, turn right between two groups of trees down a tarmac road, which is identified by an open water channel along the left hand side.

At the end of this road you will reach the *Adhari Pool* (Ain Adhari), which is now part of a landscaped national park. The water from the spring rises 10 metres into an artificially banked basin 20 metres (22 yds) x 36.6 metres (40 yds). Durand writing in the last century noted that it held "a shoal or two of large fish and many water tortoises", while Belgrave commented that "once a week in the summer, the police used to go out in lorries to bathe at Adhari, one of the biggest and deepest fresh-water springs in Bahrain".

The last section of this route is the *windtower conservation area of Al-Awadiyah*. Return to the land-mark which is pointed out at the beginning of this route, the Ibn Sinna Health Centre on the Isa Al-Kabir Road.

Turn right into Road 649. At the same time zero your kilometre gauge, then take the second right hand turn into Hoora Avenue (0.1 kms.). This is the northern boundary of the Al-Awadiyah conservation area. Proceed to the corner of Road 640 (0.3 kms.) which is distinguished by a windtower located on the junction (see Plate 112).

As the road inclines a few metres ahead, wooden balconies will be noted at the first floor level of the houses on each side of the road. The closed slats were designed to prevent the ladies of the house from being observed.

At the top of the slope turn right into Khalaf Alasfoor Avenue (0.6 kms.) and immediately right again into Road 639. As the road declines, a panorama of houses with windtowers will face you, commencing with the first example on the corner of Road 635. At 0.8 kms. the road narrows beyond the open square. At the intersection 500 metres ahead (Road 640) look to the left where other windtowers and examples of balconies will be noted. To the right, the reverse view of the first windtower noted, stands on the left side of the street.

Continue to the end of Road 639, then turn left. The Ibn Sinna Health Centre is on the right before the intersection of Isa Al-Kabir Road. Conclude the route by turning right to the "Wimpey" roundabout, and right again should you wish to return to the Hilton/Sheraton Hotels.

Plate 113: Windtowers located on Road 639.

ROUTE 6 - THE SOUTH

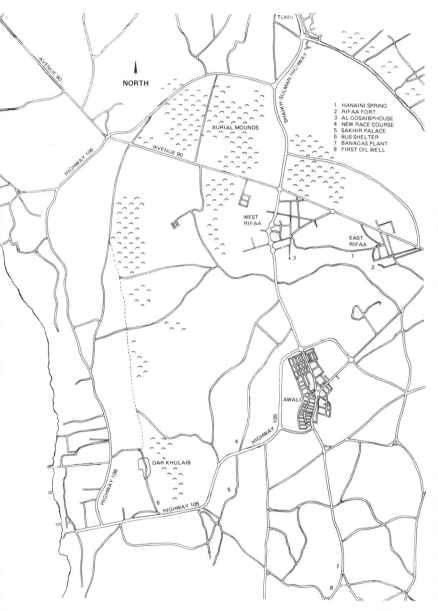

1 HANAINI SPRING
2 RIFAA FORT
3 AL-GOSAIBI HOUSE
4 NEW RACE COURSE
5 SAKHIR PALACE
6 BUS SHELTER
7 BANAGAS PLANT
8 FIRST OIL WELL

NORTH

BURIAL MOUNDS

WEST RIFAA

EAST RIFAA

AWALI

DAR KHULAIB

ROUTE 6 - THE SOUTH

The starting point for this route is the roundabout located on the Shaikh Sulman Highway, adjacent to the new Traffic Directorate Headquarters. This may be reached by following the map preceding Route 5, which starts in the centre of Manama and follows the Highway to this roundabout. Hereafter, turn to the map preceding Route 6. (As a guide, the distance from the Hilton/Sheraton Hotels to the Traffic Directorate Headquarters is 13.3 kms.)

Proceed for 2.7 kms. to the next roundabout, which marks the outskirts of the *twin towns of Rifaa*. Theodore Bent, writing in 1889, spoke of "two inland villages of Rufa'a, mountainous Rufa'a or Rufa'a Jebeli, and Rufa'a Shergeli". However, local opinion is that perhaps Bent misunderstood the pronunciation and confused the notion of a mountain (jebel) with the translation of the compass point, west (gharbi), hence his interpretation: Jebeli. The correct Arabic name is *Rifaa Al-Gharbi,* the modern town of *West Rifaa*, whilst the twin town of *East Rifaa* is known as *Rifaa Ash-Sharqi*.

Situated on a low, narrow plateau overlooking the central basin of the island, these settlements have been the traditional strongholds of the Al-Khalifa family and their allies, the Utub tribes, since the invasion of Bahrain in 1783. The two towns are close to the narrow but important pastureland of Bahrain, where the ruling family keeps its camels and stables its horses. The two Rifaas offer another obvious advantage, in that they are served by what are reputed to be the best fresh water springs in the country, those of *Hanaini* in Rifaa Ash-Sharqi, and *Umm Ghuwifa* in Rifaa Al-Gharbi. In the nineteenth and early twentieth centuries donkeys and camels laden with skin water-bags filled from these wells made the long daily trek into Manama, to provide the residents with drinking water.

West Rifaa is a modern town, built by Shaikh Sulman, the present Amir's father. The Ruler's Palace is located on the left at the second roundabout from the beginning of this route (3.7 kms.) and the Crown Prince's Majlis, completed in 1977, is on the right. Shaikh Isa bin Sulman Al-Khalifa, the Amir, is known to be very fond of gardens and so accordingly has encouraged an extensive programme of shrub and flower planting throughout the town. Oleander and bougainvillea flowers give an all-year splash of colour to the Highway, whilst the hedges cut in topiary designs provide a unique variation to roundabout decoration.

Having negotiated all the West Rifaa roundabouts, pause at the top of the escarpment, before descending the slope. From this point you will see the outline of the *Jebel Dukhan* (Mountain of Smoke). If the day is clear, the range will be clearly defined. Should the weather be hot and humid, as is often the case during the summer months, the impression may be no more than a grey, shimmering haze, hence the name. The old racecourse is located immediately at the foot of the escarpment on the left, the scene of many horse and camel races in the past.

Plate 114: Cannon on East Rifaa hill,
looking across the dip-slope to West Rifaa (horizon).
Hanaini spring is in the middle distance.

Descend the incline and proceed for a further 3.5 kms. to the oil township of **Awali**. The north gate is on the far side of the next roundabout. When the first drilling crew arrived in Bahrain in 1931, a camp was established beneath the Jebel Dukhan, some kilometres to the south. However as the oil company employees increased, it was essential to create what has now become a closely-integrated settlement, with all the modern amenities one might except, and believed to have been the first centrally air-conditioned community in the world.

Fifty years ago, there were no houses, let alone landscaped gardens. All that existed of the site was a little hillock in the middle of the desert on which it was decided to build the oil company's living accommodation, whilst the office and indusrial sectors would be built below. The area was notorious for gusting winds, and so the township was named **Mughaidrat**, (place of little dust storms). Legend has it that Shaikh Hamed, who was the Ruler at the time, felt that the name was too difficult for the non-Arabic speaking residents to pronounce. Hence on 23rd April 1938, a circular was sent to all employees:

Plate 115: Awali 1930s, prior to development.

"It has been suggested by His HIghness Shaikh Sir Hamed bin Al-Khalifa[1] that our community settlement be named Awali. We request that it be used hereafter in place of other names such as New Camp, Jebel BAPCO, or BAPCO City or any other. It will be of interest to all members of our community to know that Awali means "high place". Moreover, the entire island in early Arab times took its name from this word and was known as Awal. These associations make our adoption of the name Awali especially appropriate. Signed: C.W. Deacon."

The houses which were first built at the settlement are shown clearly in Plate 116. They were designed as bachelor accommodation which took the form of a series of rooms leading off a central corridor. Arranged at each end were the kitchen and bathrooms. The whole structure was surrounded by a verandah to provide shade from the sun, whilst the twelve feet high walls (3.65 metres) allowed for maximum circulation of air.

1 - Sh. Hamed was decorated by King Edward VIII in 1936 by being created Honorary Knight Commander of the Order of the Indian Empire (KCIE).

Plate 116: Awali houses 1930s.

Plate 117: Hoopoe Bird
"nodding-donkey" well-head.

Upon leaving Awali by the north gate, turn left at the round-about and follow Highway 105, signposted to Zellaq. Proceed to the next roundabout (2.3 kms. ahead). On your right you will note the **new racecourse** spectators' stand several hundred metres from the road. The site was opened by the Amir in March 1981, and is particularly worthy of mention since the grass is kept in perfect condition by an irrigation system which is monitored by an electronic detection system. In the event of a failure, the track can be prevented from becoming parched during the scorching heat of the summer months by quick preventative action.

On the left, 2.1 kms. further along the route, an oil-well shaped like a **Hoopoe Bird** stands back from the road (Plate 117). This is one of three well-heads which have been given a touch of humour by the oil company. The hoopoe is one of Bahrain's distinguished winter visitors readily identi-fied by the tuft of feathers on its head. The other two other animated well-heads are a giraffe and caterpillar, the latter having been designed by the Awali school children. These children. These are located on the Awali-Sitra Highway. This type of pumping-well known as a "nodding-donkey" is required where oil pressure is low.

At this point it will be possible to see a very extensive Palace complex through the trees on the left hand side of the road. This is the now abandoned **Sakhir Palace**, which during Shaikh Hamed's reign was his favourite home. Fifty years ago, it was the seat of power, controlling the government and military affairs of the country, since the town and palaces of West Rifaa had not been established at that time. It was to this country residence that the Adviser, the late Sir Charles Belgrave, would make his frequent visits from Manama, travell-ing along what was in those days just a rough track. Sir Charles recalled that the majlis was forty feet long (thirteen metres) with the walls decorated in arabesque designs cut into the plaster. The doors and window shutters were of carved teak imported from India, and the ceiling consisted of man-grove poles with a criss-cross design of split bamboos. The wooden balcony of the harem is perhaps one of the finest examples in Bahrain.

Plate 118: Sakhir Palace.

Plate 119: Mosque, Sakhir Palace.

It is the tradition in Bahrain that, upon the death of the Ruler, the house in which he passes away is closed. For this reason the residence has remained empty since 1942, when Shaikh Hamed died, and it is not open for visits. However, a fairly good impression can be gained by driving along the appropriate access road from where a view of the shaped decoration mentioned in chapter 8, part II, can be seen as well as other features such as the mosque.

1.3 kms. beyond this complex is a 400 hectare site which is marked by a large notice board. This is the proposed location for the **Arabian Gulf University** which was given the go-ahead during 1981, under the auspices of the Arab Bureau of Education for the Gulf States. Sponsored by seven Gulf nations: Bahrain, Iraq, Kuwait, Oman, Qatar, Saudi Arabia and the United Arab Emirates, it is scheduled to accommodate ten thousand students when completed in twenty years time. Enrolment is expected to start in 1986. Informed estimates put the cost at between $300 and $400 million. Another 3½ hectare site for marine research and recreational facilities is to be constructed at Ras Nawmah, south of Jeezail beach on the island's west coast.

Continuing along Highway 105 towards Zellaq, the right turn for **Dar Khulaib village** is 6.6 kms. from Awali North Gate. This is distinguished by a **bus shelter** immediately on the right after the turning. Zero your kilometre gauge upon reaching the shelter. Proceed for 1.8 kilometres through the village until you approach a sharp left hand bend. The landmark on the right will be a large water-tower. Ahead a track leads off the tarmac road where a view of the burial mounds can be gained from this point. This is the southern extremity of Route 7 and the qanat system. (See Chapter 10 also).

Return to Highway 105 and turn right. At 1.6 kms. from this turning where you rejoin the dual carriageway, a second turn to the right will lead you through the west coast villages, also marked on Route 7. Although it is not signposted at this intersection, this right turn is the **southern extremity of Highway 106**. Eventually it will join Avenue 90 (the Hamala Road), the northern extremity of Route 7.

Should you not choose to take this diversion, proceed along

Highway 105. A left turn 0.8 kms. from the Highway 106 junction leads to *Zellaq village* and the south of Bahrain island. Beyond Zellaq is the site of the *Al-Areen wild life reserve and park*, scheduled to be open to the public in 1982.

Having completed your tour of the western extremity of Route 6, return to the roundabout which preceded the Hoopoe Bird.

The new Racecourse, distinguished by a landscaped entrance, will serve as a warning landmark on the left, immediately before reaching this junction. Turn right at the roundabout's first exit. Follow the road for 1.7 kms. Take the second exit at the next roundabout, which in practice is straight ahead.

4.3 kms. from this junction you will see the *BANAGAS plant* on the left. The *Jebel Dukhan* is straight ahead. In December 1979, the Bahrain National Gas Company commissioned this plant to process gas from Bahrain's oil fields. 1980 production was 87,700 tons of propane, 74,100 tons of butane and 968,290 barrels of naphtha, with a total capacity of 280,000 tons per year of natural gas liquids. The shareholders of the plant are BANOCO (Bahrain National Oil Company) 75%, Apicorp (Arabian Petroleum Investments Corporation) 12.5% and Caltex (California Texas Oil Co. Ltd.) 12.5%.

Proceed for a further 1.3 kms. at which point you will be directly beneath the Jebel Dukhan range. The Bahrain International Communications' *Tropospheric Scatter Station* stands on a peak rising to 107 metres, behind which is the Jebel Dukhan summit (122.4 metres).

The first oil well in Bahrain is before you. This was spudded in on 16th October 1931, from which oil flowed on 1st June 1932, the initial flow-rate being 400 barrels an hour. For a description of the circumstances of its discovery, refer to Part I, chapters 2 and 4.

Whilst the development surrounding the site today is limited, fifty years ago there was nothing. When Mrs. Skinner arrived in Bahrain in October 1931 from the United States, via Bombay and the "slow mail" up the Arabian Gulf, she was the only expatriate lady in the oil company's team. When she

Plate 120: First oil well-head (foreground). Tropospheric Scatter Station (background).

reached the Jebel Camp, she found that her husband Edward, who was leading the drilling team, had established a home for them in a nissen hut (see extreme right, Plate 121). Later Mrs. Skinner was to write, "I remember well the drive out to the Jebel Camp. The date groves and gardens were beautifully kept and everything was wonderfully neat and tidy. In those days it was just a track out to the site. There was no palace at Rifa'a - in fact there were no buildings at all out there. Sakhir was the Ruler's home then.

"I had never seen a nissen hut before, but it made a splendid home - the rooms were large and it was very pleasantly furnished. None of us realised that it would ever be cold here, and what a shock we had that first winter. We hadn't brought many blankets, but Jack Schloselin built stoves from 12" (4.73 cms.) pipe for all the huts, and I think they must have saved our lives, for it was a very cold winter."

Plate 121: Jebel Camp 1934.
Mr. and Mrs. E. Skinner's home is the nissen hut on the extreme right.
The first oil well-head is also on the right.

Plate 122: Al-Gosaibi House looking towards East Rifaa.

Upon leaving this site, return to the Highway (105), turn right to Awali town north gate, take the roundabout's second exit and return to West Rifaa.

At the top of West Rifaa Hill, 2.7 kms. from the Awali north gate roundabout, turn right into Road 847. Having made the turn, look across the ridge to the right where you will see a new palatial development beside which, to the left, is the dere-lict *House of Al-Gosaibi* (Bait Al-Gosaibi), a former pearl mer-chant's home.

This can be reached by continuing along Road 847 for five hundred metres until the first roundabout. Turn right, con-tinue up the track until the road gives way to a large open space to the left of which is a football pitch. A word of caution should be offered at this point. It will be considered diplomatic to fork left across the sandy football pitch one or two hundred metres prior to the new modern complex where visitors are strongly discouraged. By approaching the Al-Go-saibi House from the east side which overlooks the ridge of Rifaa Al-Sharqi and the Hanaini Spring, visitors are less likely to provoke the anxiety of the guard at the new Palace.

Plate 123: Al-Gosaibi House.

Upon entering the courtyard of the house, it will be evident that it was a residence of some splendour in its hey-day. It was built by Abdul Aziz bin Hassan Al-Gosaibi in 1904 according to medical advice that he should live in a high, dry area. The home took about six years to complete.

In the early 1940s, the Al-Gosaibi family moved to Manama for personal reasons and visited the Rifaa house only occasionally. However, both King Abdul Aziz bin Saud, and later King Saud bin Abdul Aziz of Saudi Arabia, paid several visits to the house before the last member of the family to live there in 1950, Abdul Rahman Al-Gosaibi, finally left. Upon the death of Abdul Aziz bin Hassan Al-Gosaibi in 1953, the present Amir's father Shaikh Sulman purchased the complex. Whilst wandering around the site it is worth noting the architectural features, many of which are described in Part II, chapter 8.

Return to the little roundabout at the end of the track. Instead of turning left back along Road 847, turn right into Avenue 1. Descend a steep incline into the valley below where newly-planted oleander trees line the route. On the right side you will pass the *Hanaini spring* (Ain Hanaini) which irrigates the plants and shrubs supplied to the Municipality. A moslem cemetery on the left contains the tombstone of the former ruler Shaikh Ali, who was killed in *Rifaa Fort* after less than year in power, in 1869. This installation is situated on the edge of the escarpment to the right. (For a full story relating to the circumstances of this incident, refer to Part I, chapter 3).

Proceed up the hill to the next intersection. Turn sharp right into Shaikh Hmood bin Subah Avenue, and pass East Rifaa Health Centre on the right. Four hundred metres ahead at the top of the hill, you will approach a mosque with a single cannon in the foreground to the right.

East Rifaa is a much older town than West Rifaa which can be seen right across the valley on the opposite ridge. Its fort dominates the valley and looks out towards Awali which is to the left of your present vantage point. It was the former home of the earlier Al-Khalifa Family who ruled the islands from this place during the early nineteenth century. In recent years the town has grown as a satellite to Manama and Isa town, partly in response to the demand for more housing to accommodate employees working at the industrial developments in the south part of the island.

Little remains of the fort itself, which is now utilised as a private dwelling. Sections of decorative panels can be seen in the fort's walls as well as in those belonging to the adjacent mosque. By standing near to the cannon it is possible to appreciate the strategic position which the fort held. The locality around the fort contains typical examples of traditional architecture.

The route now concluded, you may return to Manama by retracing your steps to the East Rifaa Health Centre. Instead of turning left into the valley, continue ahead, leaving the Municipality depot on your right. Seven hundred metres beyond this little roundabout you will approach a no-entry sign. Turn right at the road island, and then left into the main Rifaa Highway on the right of which you will see the pipeline parallel to the road. Follow the Highway, past the next junction distinguished by a large water-tower on the opposite side, and proceed to the West Rifaa roundabout, recognisable as being the start of this Route. If you wish to return to Manama turn right along Shaikh Sulman Highway. If you wish to join Route 7 proceed ahead along Avenue 90.

Plate 124:
st Rifaa Fort.

ROUTE 7 - WEST

ROUTE 7 - THE WEST

The purpose of this route is to give adventurous travellers the opportunity to visit some of the least accessible sites on the island. However, complete success will depend upon the availability of time, tenacity and a four-wheel drive vehicle. It should be noted also that at the time of writing considerable change is scheduled to take place almost entirely throughout the west part of the island, therefore many of the features which are described are likely to be disturbed in the course of the next three or four years.

By studying the map preceding this route, you will note several villages down the west coast of the island. It is worth drawing attention to them for various reasons.

Jasra in the north, is a small fishing village at the present time. However, during the next two years, the lives of the inhabitants will change dramatically with the building of the eastern extremity of the Saudi Arabia-Bahrain Causeway, terminating at this coastal settlement. The main Highway linking this to the east coast of Bahrain will follow a line almost directly from the west to east across the northern sector of this Route. The village is also noted for the craft of basketmaking, especially the hand fans (mihaffa) which are made by the women in their homes and sold in the suq.

Hamala is the site of an extensive excavation which was carried out in 1968, whilst *Dumistan*, *Karzakkan* and *Al Malikiyah* villages have all witnessed archaeological activity during the course of the last half century (see relevant list, Part IV).

The west coast villages were also supplied by an *extensive qanat system* (see Part II, chapter 10) which is now derelict to a great extent and extremely hazardous in parts. This lies in a north-south axis between Avenue 90 (Hamala Road) to the north of Route 7 and Highway 105 (Awali-Zellaq Road) to the south.

The easiest way to approach the system is by taking the Dar Khulaib turnoff, indicated by the bus-shelter in the latter part of Route 6. If you are already travelling along the Hamala Road in the north, take the Highway 106 turning at the Buri village junction and follow the west coast road for 11.3 kms. south where it joins Highway 105. Turn left and follow Highway 105 for less than two kilometres at which point you will see a bus shelter on the left, set back from the road. Turn left.

Plate 125: Dar Khulaib Qanat System.

Upon approaching the bus shelter, zero your kilometre gauge. Travel for 1.8 kms., passing through Dar Khulaib village, until you reach a sharp left hand bend distinguished by a water-tank on the right. Straight ahead you will see a rough track and *a large group of burial mounds*.

Leave the tarmac road and follow the track for 1.4 kms. where you can stop and walk across the sand to inspect the cistern marked on Fig 21. At 2 kms. from leaving the tarmac road, the track follows the boundary fence of a chicken farm. Depending upon the vehicle you are using you may be fortunate enough to drive beyond the chicken farm until approximately 3.6 kms. where it will be necessary to park your vehicle in order to inspect the rest of the system. However, at the time of writing, the track was in bad shape and it is doubtful whether the majority of cars can negotiate the latter part of this section of the route. A four wheel-drive vehicle is essential if you do not wish to inspect the disused cisterns on foot.

Sections of this system are to be incorporated in to a prestigious new town which is being planned for the west coast of Bahrain. Therefore during the next few years, some of this area will be redeveloped.

Whilst a fine view of the tumuli can be gained by exploring the southern part of Route 7 and the qanat system, a more accessible vantage-point can be reached along the Hamala Road (Avenue 90).

The southern extremity of Route 5 (see relevant map) leads onto this Road. (See also the composite map with the gridded sections at the beginning of Part III.) Avenue 90 is the process of extensive modernisation and the first few kilometres are being converted into a dual carriageway.

At 2.7 kms. from the roundabout at West Rifaa, you drive over the top of a rise, giving a good view of a *large area of mounds* to the left of the road. At the time of writing there are a few excavated mounds immediately on the left at this point, but they will almost cerainly disappear as the road widening scheme progresses. From the rise the ground slopes down to a small wadi and more excavated mounds

Fig. 21: Dar Khulaib Qanat System.

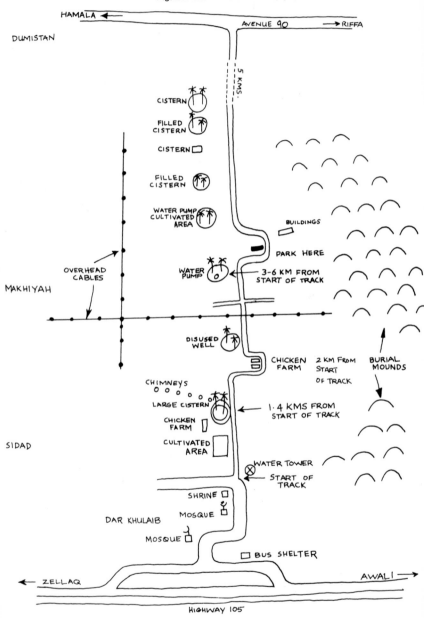

can be seen on the far side, with the gravel and sand removed and the tomb chamber and ringwall exposed. Those furthest away from the road will probably survive destruction (3 kms. from the roundabout).

Continue along Avenue 90 until 4.7 kms. At this point there is a junction signposted to Aali village (to the right) which leads to the pottery (Route 5). The left turn is signposted to Dumistan along Highway 106. Proceed ahead.

At 5.75 kilometres from the West Rifaa roundabout, the road rises up an incline. On the left there is a military camp. On the right there is a small bridge over the pipeline. Turn right and proceed along the sandy track for about 200 metres. At this point you will see more burial mounds on either side of your route which forks to the left and right.

The left fork follows the lower level of an escarpment. Continue for 2 kilometres where you will be able to see an excavated burial mound located some metres up the rise.

If you are using a four-wheel drive vehicle you will be able to drive up to the mound. Otherwise take your vehicle as far as is practical. (For those drivers who are unfamiliar with this type of terrain, care should be taken to ensure that the ground ahead is not soft sand. You will find it difficult to dig out the wheels should your car sink into the ground and at this point you are a long way from summoning help.)

The excavated burial mounds at this location represent several types of tomb (see chapter 5). A central single chamber is evident, whilst subsidiary burials can be identified around the perimeter of one of the mounds.

The ridge where these burial mounds are situated forms part of the *Saar complex* which is being excavated as part of a rescue programme before they are destroyed in preparation for the Highway which will link the Saudi Arabia-Bahrain Causeway to the east coast of the island. Whilst is it not anticipated that all of the tumuli in this area will be demolished, it is likely that those which have been described will disappear in the course of the next few years.

Upon returning to the main road, you may either return to the West Rifaa roundabout and return to Manama by the Shaikh Sulman Highway (Route 5). Or you may turn right, ascend the slope and follow the road for 5.9 kilometres, noting Avenue 6 on your left 200 metres prior to a right turn across a bridge over the pipeline into Avenue 35. By following this for five kilometres you will reach the Budaiya Highway at its western extremity (Route 8).

Plate 126: Saar Burial mound.

ROUTE 8 - BUDAIYA HIGHWAY

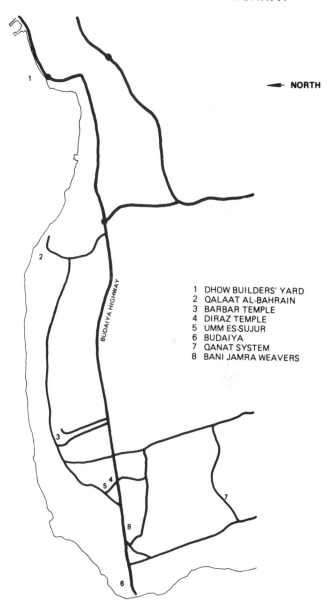

← NORTH

BUDAIYA HIGHWAY

1 DHOW BUILDERS' YARD
2 QALAAT AL-BAHRAIN
3 BARBAR TEMPLE
4 DIRAZ TEMPLE
5 UMM ES-SUJUR
6 BUDAIYA
7 QANAT SYSTEM
8 BANI JAMRA WEAVERS

ROUTE 8 - BUDAIYA HIGHWAY

This route, extending across the northern segment of Bahrain island, is distinguished by its richly endowed archaeological sites, representing Bahrain's civilisation from the 3rd millennium B.C. to the Portuguese fortifications of four hundred years ago, and by a few of the islands' traditional crafts.

As in the previous routes, take the Hilton and Sheraton Hotels as your starting point. Face the sea, proceed to the traffic lights ahead and turn left along King Faisal Highway. Having passed a second set of traffic lights and Mina Manama on your right, a roundabout at 2.6 kms. (sometimes with a fountain playing in its centre) will serve as the first major landmark. Approaching the roundabout you will observe a collection of sheds on the far right side surrounded by a perimeter fence. Instead of leaving the roundabout by the first exit, fork right across the sand towards the shore and the collection of wood and wire assembled near the buildings.

The Dhow Builders' Yards is one of the two locations in Bahrain where wooden boat building is practised still and visitors may observe craftsmen constructing the vessels using no plans, no mechanised instruments (although some of the dhow builders now use electrically powered tools) and imported wood from India. For a full description of the method of construction, refer to Part II, chapter 9. Wire fish-traps are also made at this location, and may be seen piled on the decks of dhows when the fishing fleet is in harbour.

Having visited the Dhow Builders' Yards return to the roundabout. Turn right and proceed to the traffic lights ahead, just past an archway across the road. Fork right prior to the intersection (3.5 kms.) to join the Budaiya Highway.

Within 350 metres you will note derelict structures on the central reservation. These are reputed to be former mosques which were built in the days when the Highway was a track leading from the nearby villages to the date-groves on each side of the present road. Since it was then too far for the farmers to travel home for midday prayers, these mosques provided appropriate alternative places of worship to those in their villages.

Continue along the Highway, through the village of Jidhafs (5.5 kms.), through a set of traffic lights (6.2 kms.) to a roundabout at 6.7 kms. Turn right 250 metres beyond this landmark. (Should you pass the main gate of the International Hospital on your right, you have gone too far.) Follow the road for 0.8 kms. which is signposted to the Bahrain Fort, fork right and proceed to 1.2 kms. where the road bends sharply to the right, and then left. At 2 kms. from where you left the Budaiya Highway, there is a T-junction with Karbabad Avenue signposted to the right. Make this turn, reset your kilometre gauge and proceed for 200 metres. Between the trees on the right, you will see a rough track leading to a glade. Leave your vehicle beside the road and walk along this path to where the *Karbabad Basket Makers* sit weaving their wares in the shade of their palmleaf shelters. One of the craftsmen may be seen splitting the asig, the branch on which the dates grow, into long strips. The split lengths are then used for the foundation strengthening in the circular baskets, as it is the coarsest part of the palm tree, other than the trunk. When the foundation has been made, it is then bound with softer, more pliable strips of palm-frond. Some-times this has been dyed purple or green with chemicals bought in the Suq to create decorative sections in the baskets.

Plate 127: Chicken coops and baskets, Karbabad.

The traditional dining manner in Bahrain is to place a circular woven mat (sofrah) on the floor, upon which the food dishes are arranged so that the family may squat round in a circle to eat their meal. These mats can be seen hanging on the barasti walls of the weavers' huts, ready for sale. Chicken coops (chiseh) and smaller versions for carrying little birds are made from asig and may be purchased for a few dinars. These take about three hours to make, whilst the woven date baskets with lids (saleh rubat) may take as long as three days to weave, depending upon the complexity of the coloured palm variation chosen for the design. The large, flat, open date dishes without lids (sabog) takes a little less time.

It should come as no surprise therefore to discover that these vessels are proportionately more expensive than the bird coops. Unfortunately, attempting to drive too hard a bargain tends to prompt a demand for money in return for taking photographs and watching the basket makers at work.

After your visit return to the T-junction 200 metres from the main road. Instead of retracing your route to the left, turn right, and ascend the tell (city mound) ahead.

QALAAT AL-BAHRAIN is the oldest known city complex of Bahrain. It is often referred to as the Portuguese Fort or Bahrain Fort (Qalaat Al-Bahrain), but both of these names are misleading since the site which you are now looking at covers 7 stratified levels of occupation which range from the third millennium B.C. to the 16th century A.D. Excavated material is on display in the museum.

The first five levels are the least evident and the most widely dispersed. They extend to the far west, the south, the east, and a large excavated area E (Fig. 22) to the south-east of the Portuguese Fort (city level VII).The sixth city level is adjacent to the shore to the north, where excavation is being undertaken currently by the French expedition, led by Dr. Monik Kervran. This consists of an Islamic Fort probably dating to the 11th century. The seventh level is the 16th century Portuguese Fort after which the site takes its name, since its prominent bastions were the only visible remains of the complete site complex until twenty-five years ago, prior to excavation.

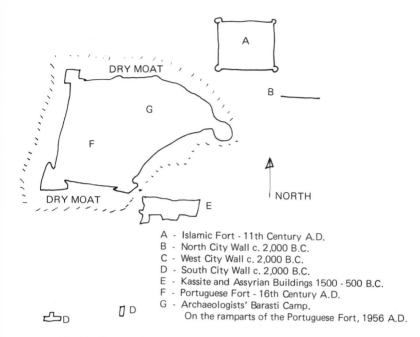

SEA

DRY MOAT

A

B _____

G

F

DRY MOAT

E

NORTH

A - Islamic Fort - 11th Century A.D.
B - North City Wall c. 2,000 B.C.
C - West City Wall c. 2,000 B.C.
D - South City Wall c. 2,000 B.C.
E - Kassite and Assyrian Buildings 1500 - 500 B.C.
F - Portuguese Fort - 16th Century A.D.
G - Archaeologists' Barasti Camp.
    On the ramparts of the Portuguese Fort, 1956 A.D.

D   D

Fig. 22: Diagram of Qalaat Al-Bahrain.

The remains of the Danish archaeologists' camp built in 1956 can be found on the upper ramparts of the 16th century fort. Geoffrey Bibby, co-leader of the Danish expedition, humourously refers to this as City VIII[1] , consisting of a "jumble of some dozen barastis on the edge of the tell, and a foreign intrusive culture, a Danish settlement, within the ramparts of City VII. We forthwith entitled ourselves the Carlsberg culture."[2]

It was also in 1956, the third year of excavation, that Bibby together with Professor P.V. Glob, worked out the Seven-City sequence as a result of various sondages (deep test digs) and limited, structured excavation. Cities 1 to 4 are all different stages of the civilization now known as Dilmun.

1 - G. Bibby, Looking for Dilmun, p. 169.
2 - The Carlsberg Foundation, based in Denmark, sponsored the expedition.

City I is of uncertain date, although it is believed that the first dwellings were constructed c. 2,800 B.C. The small and apparently unfortified assemblage of stone-built houses are overlaid by the massive fortifications of the second city, although sufficient evidence remains to suggest that the city was sacked and burnt c. 2,300 B.C. by an army of Sargon the Great.

City II was a fortified settlement, the remains of which can be seen at three points around the perimeter of the tell (see Fig. 22). The outher walls, probably of a later date, appear to have been set in gypsum, although much of the original facing stones have disappeared, perhaps quarried for the construction of City V. The second city was probably founded immediately after the sack of the first, c. 2,300 B.C. and survived for approximately five hundred years.

The excavations in area B have exposed part of the city wall, including the north gate, through which sea-borne trade would have passed. Two levels of building are clear, the lower one belonging to City II, with a rough stone wall and single gateway. This period is contemporary with the majority of the grave mounds and with the main Barbar Temple. It was in this area of the city gate that a number of important finds were made, including stamp seals, copper fragments and a set of stone weights identical to some already found in the Indus Valley cities, which indicate that Bahrain was at that time the centre of trade in the Gulf and therefore in all probability, Dilmun.

City III is the third phase of building at Qalaat Al-Bahrain. This took place around 1800 B.C. The upper level of the city wall exposed at area B, characterised by a plastered surface and three gateways, each faced with cut limestone slabs belongs to this period. A few more remains from this period, in the form of large, heavy wall-footings beneath later buildings, are visible in area E.

A radio-carbon date c. 1190 B.C. suggests that the City III buildings were destroyed by a conflagration, a theory supported by the evident sootmarks on the masonry. City III pottery is identical with that which was in use in Mesopotamia during this period, namely the Kassite Period (see Part II, chapter 6). Unfortunately, cuneiform texts have little to say about Dilmun during this time, and much more needs to be known.

Plate 128: Qalaat Al-Bahrain complex. Section of the excavated site.

City IV is represented by the most imposing ruins of all in this section of the excavations (area E). Dating from between 900 and 600 B.C., the period when the Assyrians had moved south to occupy Mesopotamia, the excavated buildings represent a large house or "palace". A small lane leads to a massive entrance, the doorway of which stands over three metres high and is constructed from finely cut blocks of limestone quarried from Jidda island. This doorway is clearly Assyrian in style. Note the curve in the wall beside it to allow the door to swivel open.

The entrance gives onto a small courtyard, with the bases of pillars still visible. Inside the house are three bathrooms, each with a drainage system, indicating a fairly high level of comfort and standard of engineering at this period.

Archaeological finds here include "snake-burials": a number of covered pottery bowls, each containing the remains of a snake and a semi-precious stone, discovered beneath the floor of the courtyard. It has been suggested that they are perhaps a survival of the Gilgamesh legend of the snake which achieved immortality at the expense of mankind.

A hoard of silver and a bath-tub shaped coffin of Assyrian type were also found in this area. The silver hoard perhaps suggests a sudden disaster; certainly after this period there are no more known references to Dilmun, and it is suggested that the Assyrians extended their conquests to include Bahrain at about this time.

City V refers to the Greek period of occupation of this site. There was a settlement here at the time of Alexander the Great and of his successor, General Seleucus, who together with his family eventually controlled Asia Minor and the part of Arabia which included Bahrain (approximately from 300 to 0 B.C.).

Little in the way of building has been found, but terracottas and pottery associated with the Seleucid Dynasty were excavated here and at Al-Hajjar (also in·this route). The associated Attic ware indicates that trade flourished with the Greek empire.

234.

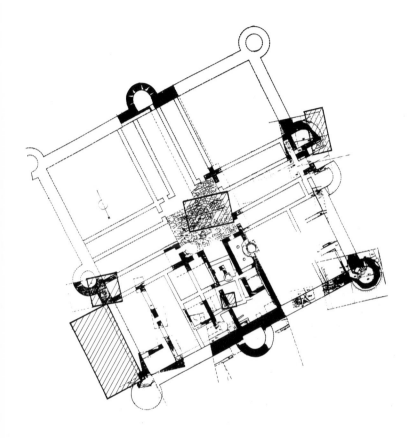

Fig. 23. Layout of Islamic Fort Qalaat Al-Bahrain.

Plate 129: Islamic Fort, Qalaat Al-Bahrain.

City VI is represented by an 11th century A.D. Islamic fort (A on the plan). It was first discovered by Geoffrey Bibby during the Danish expedition's work, and during the last three years has been excavated by Dr. Kervran assisted by a team of French archaeologists.

Dr. Kervran, in a preliminary report, ascribes the fort to the Carmathians, an Islamic sect which flourished from the 9th-11th centuries A.D. and had their headquarters at Hofuf, in Saudi Arabia. Their warlike tradition is borne out by the purely military function of the building.

The fort is square, with towers at each corner and half-towers in the middle of each side, except on the west, where two quarter-towers frame the main gate. Strategically sited arrow slits ensured defence. The interior is planned around a paved courtyard. The walls were faced with good quality stone, much of which was later used in the construction of the Portuguese Fort, but without decoration.

Few dateable artefacts have so far been found, apart from weapons, including a pile of stones coated with naphtha, used for setting fire to targets. Later levels yielded chinese coins and porcelain of the 14th and 15th centuries, but the site was not built on subsequently.

This fort is possibly the oldest example of a fortified building in a region where this type of architecture was at that time unknown. The style may have been from Syria, where the Byzantine tradition of building forts was carried on by architects of the Ummayid period.

City VII is ascribed to the 16th century, the period when the Portuguese ruled Bahrain for approximately eighty years. Two factors are believed to have been the impetus for the Fort's construction, the uneasy hold of the Portuguese over the allegiance of the local population and the increasing conflict with the Ottomans for hegemony of the Gulf in 1550 A.D.

In 1602, the Portuguese were ousted by the Persians, who had been strengthening their armies over the previous decade. Until the end of the 16th century a series of Persian governors ruled Bahrain with the aid of a garrison stationed at the Fort.

By the turn of the century the Omanis invaded Bahrain and built Arad Fort. From this time, Bahrain Fort (Qalaat Al-Bahrain) is thought to have declined in strategic importance.

The fort itself comprises three high, massive bastions in varying, but relatively good preservation, parts of two higher central towers, and long stretches of heavily decayed walls linking the bastions. The whole outline of the moat and fortress is visible, but the east towers are ruined.

Four rooms and three staircases within the bastions are well preserved. The other rooms cannot be entered although an idea of their structure can be observed obliquely through holes in the roof of the southwest bastion. However, a word of caution should be offered to this point. As the roof is of a domed construction it is extremely dangerous to walk too close to the edge of the holes since the entire structure is liable to collapse with unsupported weight.

Plate 130: South Bastion of the Portuguese Fort.

Of the six rooms, five are roofed with domes on squinch arches above semidomes. The sixth room is roofed with a barrel vault carried on transverse arches. All of the rooms have a large arched firing port, the actual opening in each case being reduced to a narrow square. The two rooms in the northern bastion have, in addition, divided firing ports to allow fire raking.

In its final form, the fortress had its major defensive works in a roughly square plan on the eastern side, with a triangular outer bailey to the west. Access was apparently across an arched causeway from the south, through the outer bailey, and through a gate in what is now almost the centre of the mound, facing west, and thus into a large central courtyard. The largest bastions are those on the northwest, the southeast and in the centre of the south side. There was a further wide, but low, bastion at the eastern end of the outer bailey.

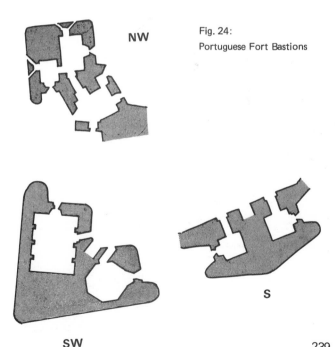

NW

Fig. 24:
Portuguese Fort Bastions

S

SW

As mentioned earlier, the remains of the Danish archaeologists' barasti camp are still evident in the centre of the fort. (For a description of its construction, refer to chapter 7.) A collection of cannon balls from the Portuguese magazine lie near one of the huts.

On leaving the Portuguese Fort, return to the Budaiya Highway and turn right, and zero your kilometre gauge. After 1.4 kms. a partially excavated site is situated beside the Highway on the right. This is a settlement called *Al-Migsha'a* which has produced evidence of the Hellenistic period, similar to that found at Al-Hajjar. In 1978, a rescue archaeology operation was carried out by the Department of Antiquities on another part of the site, where an electricity sub-station has been built since. However, before the section was obliterated, enough material had been documented to indicate that a small Islamic Fort had been part of the Al-Migsha'a settlement.

Plate 131: Barasti shelter on the ramparts of Qalaat Al-Bahrain. Note Portuguese cannon balls.

Proceed along the Budaiya Highway for a further 2.7 kms, past Ashraf's Saveway Supermarket and past the turning to Jawad Superfare (both on the right). At 4.3 kms on your gauge look out for a right turn, signposted to the Barbar Temple. Make the turn and continue along this road for 0.8 kms. until you note a mound on the right, 150 metres from the road. This is the *Barbar Temple* complex which was excavated by the Danish expedition in the 1950s at the same time as Qalaat Al-Bahrain. Only parts of the later building phases remain exposed, since the majority of the site was back-filled in order to preserve the monument.

The top of the tell is distinguished by the inner wall of a square complex which surrounds a courtyard, still partially paved with sandstone flags. Part of this was a double-plinth, two rings of stones framed in a raised oblong. When the central court had been cleared during excavation, three standing stones with holes pierced through them were found, suggesting that sacrificial animals had probably been tethered to these points. One of them bore a bull's head carved in the round, substantiating the view that the site was a temple complex. This terrace proved to be the upper level of a third building phase, beneath which were the floors of two earlier temples.

Plate 132: Upper terrace of Barbar Temple.

It is believed that the first temple was erected c. 2,800 B.C. on a simple mound of clay. Subsequently this was demolished and a second temple was constructed on a larger and higher mound with a stone terrance and walls. At the western end a flight of steps led down to a walled tank, the remains of which are visible. Perhaps this was used for baptism or in purification rites, but in any event it was not the only water supply to the temple since another well lay by the head of the staircase. The tank may have been a "wishing well" or a communication channel to the god of the nether waters, for it contained seven of the round stamp seals mentioned in Part II, chapter 6.

Plate 133: Barbar Temple walled tank.

Temple III was an even grander construction, whose larger walls are of chiselled ashlar masonry, quarried from the island of Jidda. These stretched out to enclose a spring to the north with two stone plinths marking the probable entrance.

It is believed that the three construction phases may be attributed to the same people, living not many generations apart. Pottery characterised by round pots of red ware with horizontal ridges were found in all occupation levels of the site and it is after the name of this temple complex that the now famous Barbar ware takes its name. Of the most impressive

Plate 134: Diraz temple site.

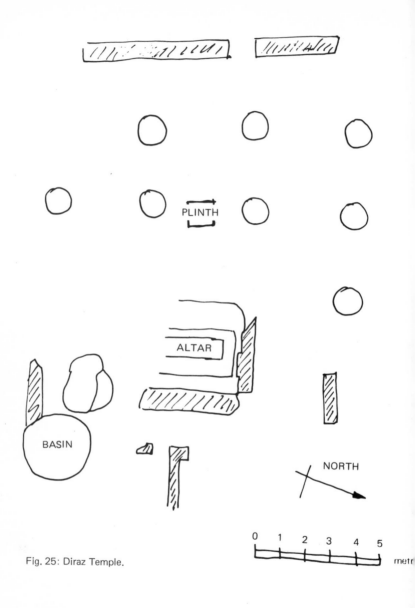

PLINTH

ALTAR

BASIN

NORTH

0 1 2 3 4 5
metr

Fig. 25: Diraz Temple.

Key wall
⌀ Column bases

244

artefacts to be found in a heap of discarded copper bands and sheeting in the Temple II courtyard, was a magnificient bull's head of copper, and a figurine of a bird, both of which are displayed in the Museum, Route 2, together with plans and photographs of the various stages of the temple.

Return to the Budaiya Highway, and turn right. Proceed for 0.7 kilometre, at which point the turning to Bar Bar Supermarket is indicated to the right. 500 metres beyond this turn on the same side of the road you will note a dried up wadi and a perimeter fence on a slight rise. Leave your vehicle and walk up the incline to enter the *Diraz Temple site*.

Michael Roaf, the Field Director during the 1976 excavation, commented that the plan of this temple is quite different to that of the Barbar Temple and is not similar to those of Mesopotamia or the Indus valley in the third and second millennia B.C. "The identification of the building as a temple is certain, but the nature of the god or gods to whom it might be dedicated is still a mystery."

Upon entering the site a room is located on the left (west), perhaps even a house, at the far end of which a door-post hole remains in the ground. A series of circular column bases of stone rubble bound with gypsum mortar and faced with a very hard white gypsum plaster present a plan of great interest. Generally, the column bases are 1m 20 cm. in diameter 2 to 3 metres apart, standing to a maximum height of 60 cm. In the centre of the second row a square altar or cult-statue plinth with slightly sloping sides is located.

The centre of the building was occupied with a cella which was open to the west by way of a low step 10 cm. high with the mark of a circular object left in the plaster. Whether this is an altar or pillar impression is uncertain. The inner area of the cella contains an altar with a sacrificial drain-hole in the floor. At the cella's southern end a damaged ablution bowl is located, whilst to the east there is a destroyed grave which apparently dates to the second millennium B.C. Dr. McNicholl, the excavation director, found a snake bowl and two stamp seals with carved animal designs, one a rampant gazelle, in the eastern store room. Other interesting artefacts were two small pots of Barbar ware with applique clay collars, these having been added later as the name suggests. The site has been restored to some extent, both as a protection and to make its layout clearer to visitors.

Upon leaving this site turn right 100 metres ahead. Follow the road for 800 metres. The location of the next site is not immediately apparent from the road However, if you look out for a place where there is a slight mound with thorn trees growing on its summit, this will be a guide. If you reach the right-hand turning to Barbar Supermarket which is 900 metres from the Budaiya Highway, you will have gone too far.

Upon leaving the car walk for about 30 yards towards the mound where it will be possible to see the next location by comparing your vantage point with Plate 135. This illustrates a series of large slabs lying on the ground and a white faced house in the far distance.

Plate 135: Umm Es-Sujur Site.

Ain Umm Es-Sujur was, at the beginning of the Islamic era, the largest of the three most important springs in Bahrain. During the 7th century, the capital city of the island was situated adjacent to the Ain Umm Es-Sujur. Tradition has it that Caliph Abd-el Malik ibn Marwan (685-705 A.D.) came to Bahrain with an invading army, and after a long and indecisive war assassinated the leaders of Bahrain, won mastery over the island and punished the inhabitants for their lapse from Islam by destroying the spring of Umm Es-Sujur, which has never been reopened. However, the Danish expedition, which excavated the site in the 1950s, found something rather different.

The spring lay in an oval hollow, roughly 70 x 40 metres and surrounded by high sandbanks, the sides and tops of which are scattered with approximately one hundred carefully cut stone blocks (illustrated in Plate 135). Some of these are a metre long, rectangular, with additional rivets and "door-post" holes, particularly significant since squared building stone is very rare in Bahrain. Excavation gave several positive results.

In the slope of the southeast corner of the hollow parallel walls with a sloping ramp between them were excavated to reveal a staircase which led down to a small well-chamber. When cleared, the well flowed again. In the eastern wall of the chamber was a little niche measuring 33 x 36 cms. and 40 cms. deep.

A decapitated limestone statue of a kneeling animal was found by the west wall. A second headless animal statue was found on a well step, whilst a little oblong stone block hollowed at the top resembled the small incense braziers of wood covered with iron sheeting in which Arabs burn sandalwood. In addition, part of an alabaster bowl and a number of pottery fragments were found, the pottery being of the Barbar type (c. 2000 B.C.). It is therefore possible that this well is the reason for the site of the Diraz Temple. It is also interesting to speculate whether the tradition of destruction in the 7th century A.D. is correct, or whether there was more than one destruction of the well. In any event, this tiny well-chamber cannot have been built as part of an ordinary system of water-supply. The evidence suggests that the little water-temple was associated with the religion current on the island prior to the coming of Islam.

Return to Budaiya Highway once more, and turn right. Reset the kilometre gauge. Proceed for 2.0 kms. to the *Experimental Gardens* on the right side. If you happen to pass by during their opening hours which are advertised on the signboard outside, they are well worth a visit. Continuing past the gardens' gateway, the Budaiya Public Security Post is 300 metres ahead, just before the road intersection. It is worth noting that the stall facing you at this point sells excellent fresh fruit drinks.

Budaiya village was the home of the Dawasir tribe in the early nineteenth century which subsequently became wealthy as a result of their pearl-diving activities. When they left Bahrain for political reasons earlier this century to settle in Saudi Arabia, the village was deserted for a while. Eventually, it was resettled by other Bahrainis and their houses are now widely scattered throughout the district. North of Budaiya is the Abu Subh beach, a popular bathing and picnic spot for Bahraini residents. Before leaving the village it is worth making a diversion to the little pier, from where it is possible to see Umm An-Nassan and Jidda islands.

Leave Budaiya village and return along the Budaiya Highway for 0.4 kms. Turn right into Avenue 55, just beyond the Experimental Gardens. Continue along this road for 3.0 kms. and then turn left.

Plate 136: Qanat System, off Avenue 55.

The next location is the northern extremity of the **Qanat system**, mentioned in Part II, chapter 10. At 4.0 kms. the road bends sharply to the right and then to the left over a little bridge. This is in fact where the road crosses the qanat system. By referring to Plate 136 you will recognise the "chimney" or head of the ventilation shaft of the system, a few examples of which can be seen for a few hundred metres at this point. For a full description of their function, refer to chapter 10.

Return to the Budaiya Highway. Turn right and proceed for 400 metres, to where the village of Bani Jamra is signposted to the right. Turn right and fork left and proceed to the village.

The Bani Jamra Weavers operate in thirteen workshops throughout the village. The first one is on a slight rise 200 metres from the main road. The barasti shelters where the craftsmen work are easily identified, and on the whole the weavers welcome interest shown in their work.

The most usual products are the lengths of black cloth which are woven for the irdeh, worn as a type of abbayah by the women. These are made as lengths of black cloth, with a band of red and gold interwoven at each end. Another type of cloth is brightly checked, and worn by men as a kind of kilt.

Plate 137: Bani Jamra weaver's shelter.

The cotton weaving threads are imported from China and India, whilst the gold lame is made in Taiwan. As Plate 138 demonstrates, the cotton threads, wound into a large skein, are secured some distance from the shelter inside a bag. These form the warp.

When the required length of fabric has been woven, it is cut from the loom and taken out into the open to be secured to a stretcher, ready for starching (Plate 139).

By studying Plate 138, it will become obvious why the weaver uses such extensive skeins of cotton for threading the warp. Since it takes many days of non-productivity to complete this task, the weaver is able to save time by using large skeins, thus enabling him to weave several lengths of cloth by gradually letting out the required amount of cotton. At the same time he must ensure that the threaded warp is secured when each finished length of cloth is cut from the loom.

Plate 138: Weaving loom, Bani Jamra.

Upon leaving Bani Jamra return to Manama by way of the Budaiya Highway. At 5.6 Kms. from the Bani Jamra turning you will note a group of burial mounds on the right, several hundred metres from the road. This is the *Al-Hajjar* site.

This is thought to belong chiefly to the Seleucid period, and artefacts found here, including glassware and seals, may be seen at the Museum (Route 2).

For those interested, it is possible to walk to the mounds after driving for a short distance across the rough track. It must be said that little remains of the excavation in situ, the graves being on the whole so deep that many were back-filled following excavation. A commentary relating to the burial and pottery type appears in chapters 5 and 6.

Plate 139: Children preparing finished cloth on a stretcher for starching.

PART IV: AIDS & SUPPLEMENTS

PROFILES

BAHRAIN HISTORICAL & ARCHAEOLOGICAL SOCIETY

The Society was originally formed in 1953 but was inactive from 1959 until January 1970 when it was re-organized to coincide with the Third International Conference on Asian Archaeology, held in Bahrain in March 1970. Since then it has been consistently active and works closely with the Directorate of Antiquities.

The Society's aims are to promote and encourage the study of and interest in the history and archaeology of Bahrain and the Gulf region and to help preserve the islands' ancient monuments. Its activities include lectures, discussions and visits to archaeological sites, and it has been involved in several exhibitions over the past decade. It is also responsible for the welfare of visiting archaeologists and runs an active schools' programme, introducing children to the culture and history of Bahrain. The Society publishes a journal, the "Dilmun Magazine" and in 1977 produced a film, entitled "Pictures of an Island", with the help of a grant from the Ministry of Information.

Since 1980 the BHAS has had its own premises in Jufair, thanks to the generosity of the Ministry of Information. This has enabled the Society to build up a reference library, which is open to members and visitors before meetings and by arrangement. Lectures and other special events are held in the main hall of the clubhouse.

The 1981-1982 executive committee of the Society is as follows:

Dr. Abdul Latif Kanoo, President
Dr. Mohammed Al Khosai, Vice President
Joan A. Porter, Secretary
Norbert Papali, Treasurer
Leslie Currie, Assistant Treasurer
Shaikh Isa bin Moh'd Al Khalifa
Khalid Zayani
Ahmed Kaiksow
Jean Hirst

Sub-committee members (non-elective):

Library: Jean Williams
Schools' Programme: Shelby Mamdani
Visiting Archaeologists: Marion Bowman
Dilmun Magazine: Chris Greenfield
Publicity: Yusuf Hubaishi

The Society has approximately 200 members at the time of publication of the guidebook. Anyone wishing to become a member of the Society is invited to apply for a membership form to the BHAS, P.O. Box 5087, Manama, Bahrain.

1981 subscriptions per annum: Family BD 6.000; Single BD 4.000; Student BD 2.000. The BHAS year runs from October 1 to June 30.

COMMITTEE FOR EAST ARABIAN AND GULF STUDIES

The Committee was formed in London in 1971 to encourage and promote archaeological work in the area of the Arabian Gulf, particularly Bahrain. It has sponsored four seasons' of excavation in Bahrain, during which time 70 sites have been surveyed and sondages made at four of them. Three sites in particular have been excavated extensively:
Al-Markh, Diraz East and Aali East.

The present officers of the Committee are:

Chairman: Dr. R.D. Barnett, 14 Eldon Grove, London NW3, United Kingdom

Vice Chairman: Professor David Oates, Institute of Archaeology, University of London, London WC1, United Kingdom

Hon. Secretary   Dr. J.E. Curtis, Department of Western
and Treasurer: Asiatic Antiquities, The British Museum, London WC1B 3DG, United Kingdom

EXCAVATIONS CONDUCTED IN BAHRAIN

1878/9	Aali Mounds	Captain E.L. Durand
1889	Aali Mounds	Theodore Bent
1903	Unspecified Mound	M. Jouannin
1906/8	67 Mounds	Captain F.B. Prideaux
1923/6	Aali Mounds et al	Ernest Mackay
1940/4	Archaeological Survey	Dr. Peter B. Cornwall
1953/70	Bahrain Fort Barbar Aali	The Danish Expedition led by Professor P.V. Glob and Geoffrey Bibby
1968	Hamala North - one - storeyed tumulus	Mrs. E.P. Jefferson
	47 miscellaneous mounds	Captain R. Higham
1969/70	Ash-Shakhoura	Antiquities Division (formed in 1968 under the Directorate of Education) Dr. Abdul Kader Takriti
1969/74	Al-Hajjar - Sites 1 & 2	" "
1970/1	Diraz Village	" "
1971/3	Umm Al-Hassam Abu Ashira	" "
1972/3	Jidhafs group	" "
1973	Grave site near Moon Plaza	" "
	Mahooz Date Garden (27 graves)	" "
	Abu Ashira (56 graves)	" "
	Preliminary Survey	Dr. A.W. McNicholl
1973/4	Al-Markh	Joint Expedition: Antiquities Division and Committee for Arabian and Gulf Studies

256

1975	Al-Migsha'a	Antiquities Division
1976	Al-Markh Diraz Aali East Quraiya North	Joint-Expedition: Dept. of Antiquities and Committee for Arabian Gulf Studies Dr. M. Roaf
1976	Al-Khamis Mosque	UNESCO
1977	Saar	Arab Expedition of Rescue Archaeology (combined UNESCO operation with representatives from 3 to 5 countries)
1978	Diraz Temple Aali Mounds	Joint Bahraini-British expedition Dr. M. Roaf
	Jidhafs	Department of Antiquities
	Harbour of the Islamic Fort (Qalaat Al-Bahrain)	Danish Expedition
	Karzakaan Mounds	Department of Antiquities
	Islamic Fort (Qalaat Al-Bahrain)	Joint Bahraini-French Expedition led by Dr. M. Kervran
	Al-Migsha'a	Department of Antiquities Rescue Archaeology "dig"
	Arad Fort	Joint Bahraini-French Expedition
1978/9	Abu Mahur Fort	Department of Antiquities excavation followed by restoration by Ministry of the Interior
1979/80	Saar and Ash-Shakhoura	Joint-Expedition: Department of Antiquities and Australian team led by D. Petocz

1979	Umm Jidr	Joint-Expedition: Department of Antiquities and French team led by J-F Salles
1980//1	Janussan	"
1980	Saar	Department of Antiquities
	Al-Malqea	"
1981	Saar	" led by Dr. Mohd. Rafique Mughal
1981	Buri Village (site of new town) West Rifaa	" "
	Islamic Fort	Joint-Expedition: Department of Antiquities and French team led by Dr. M. Kervran

APPENDICES

ABBREVIATIONS

Apicorp   Arab Petroleum Investments Corporation

ASRY   Arab Ship Repairing Yard

BANOCO   Bahrain National Oil Company

BAPCO   Bahrain Petroleum Company Ltd.

BDF   Bahrain Defence Force

BHAS   Bahrain Historical and Archaeological Society

BMA   Bahrain Monetary Agency

CALTEX   California Texas Oil Company Ltd.

GCC   Gulf Co-operation Council

OAPEC   Organisation of Arab Petroleum Exporting
           Countries

OBU   Offshore Banking Unit

OPEC   Organisation of Petroleum Exporting Countries

SOCAL   Standard Oil Company of California

UNESCO   United Nations Educational, Scientific and Cul-
           tural Organisation

BIBLIOGRAPHY

Albarn, K., Jenny Miall Smith, Stanford Steele, Dinah Walker, THE LANGUAGE OF PATTERN, Thames and Hudson (London) 1974

Al-Oraifi, R. ARCHITECTURE OF BAHRAIN, Tourist Gallery (Bahrain) 1978

Al-Takriti, Dr. Abdul Kader "Diraz Excavation and its Chronological Position" A talk to the B.H.A.S., April 1973 DILMUN 4, June 1973

Al-Tarawneh, Fayez PRELIMINARY REPORT ON SHAKHOURA EXCAVATIONS BAHRAIN, 1.10.69 - 31.12.69, B.H.A.S. Library

Al-Tarawneh, Fayez A REPORT ON AL-HAJJAR EXCAVATIONS, Mound No. 1, B.H.A.S. Library

Bahadori, Mehdi N. "Passive Cooling Systems in Iranian Architecture", SCIENTIFIC AMERICAN, Vol. 238 (2), February 1978

Belgrave, Sir Charles PERSONAL COLUMN, Hutchinson (London) 1960; re-printed by Librairie du Liban (Beirut) 1972

Belgrave, Sir Charles "The Portuguese in the Bahrain Islands" JOURNAL OF THE ROYAL CENTRAL ASIAN SOCIETY, 1935

Belgrave, James H.D. WELCOME TO BAHRAIN, The Augustan Press (Bahrain) 1953; 9th ed. 1975

Bent, J. Theodore "The Bahrain Islands in the Persian Gulf" PROCEEDINGS OF THE ROYAL GEOGRAPHIC SOCIETY, XII, 1890

Bibby, Geoffrey "Arabian Gulf Archaeology", KUML, Arborg for Jysk Arkaeologisk Selskab 1964, with summaries in English Universitetsforlaget 1 Arhus, 1965

Bibby, Geoffrey D.H. Gordon, Sir Mortimer Wheeler, "The Ancient Indian Style Seals from Bahrain", ANTIQUITY, XXXII, 1958 pp. 243-246

Bibby, Geoffrey "Arabian Gulf Archaeology", KUML, Arborg for Jysk Arkaeologisk Selskab 1965, with summaries in English Universitetsforlaget 1 Arhus, 1966

Bibby, Geoffrey LOOKING FOR DILMUN, Collins (London) 1970; Pelican Books (London) 1972, re-printed 1980

Bibby, Geoffrey "The Well of the Bulls", KUML, Arborg for Jysk Arkaeologisk Selskab 1954, with summaries in English Universitetsforlaget 1 Arhus, 1955

Bonnenfant, Paul and Guillemette, Salim ibn Hamad ibn Sulayman Al-Harthi "Architecture and Social History and Mudayrib" THE JOURNAL OF OMAN STUDIES, Vol. 3, Part 2, 1977 pp. 107-36

Bray, Warwick, David Trump THE PENGUIN DICTIONARY OF ARCHAEOLOGY, Penguin Books (London) 1970

Chappell, Herbert ARABIAN FANTASY, Quartet Books (London) 1976

Cleuziou, Serge, Pierre Lombard, Jean-Francois Salles, "Fouilles a Umm Jidr" Bahrain Recherche sur les Grandes Civilisations. Memoire No. 7.
C.N.R.S. (Centre des Recherches Archeologiques U.R.A. No. 30, Edition A.D.P.F. (Paris) 1981

Clingly, John "Archaeological Aspects of the Howar Islands" DILMUN, No. 1, December 1971

Clingly, John "Exploring Bahrain's Qanats" DILMUN, 1974

Coady, Marguerite (Ed) "Before Dilmun and After" B.H.A.S. News-ketter, No. 4, June 1973

Coles, Anne, Peter Jackson "Windtowers" Aarp - Art and Archaeology Research Papers (London)

Cornwall, Dr. Peter B. DILMUN: THE HISTORY OF BAHRAIN IS-LAND BEFORE CYRUS (A Thesis submitted in partial fulfill-ment for the Ph.D. degree at Harvard University) Cambridge, Mass. (USA), September 1944

Cornwall, Dr. Peter B. "In Search of Arabia's Past" NATIONAL GEO-GRAPHIC MAGAZINE, April 1948

Cornwall, Dr. Peter B. "On the Location of Dilmun" BULLETIN OF AMERICAN SCHOOL OF ORIENTAL RESEARCH, No. 103, 1946 pp. 3-11

Cornwall, Dr. Peter B. "The Tumuli of Bahrein" ASIA AND THE AMERICAS, Vol. XLIII, April 1943

Doornkamp, J.C., D. Brunsden, D.K.C. Jones (Ed.) "Geology, Geomor-phology and Pedology of Bahrain" GEO ABSTRACTS LTD., University of East Anglia, Norwich U.K. 1980

Durand, Capt. E.L. "The Islands and Antiquities of Bahrain" (with notes by Maj. - Gen. Sir H.C. Rawlinson) JOURNAL OF THE ROYAL ASIATIC SOCIETY (New Series), XII, (Part II) 1880, pp. 189-227

During Caspers, Dr. Elisabeth C.L. 'A Dilmunite Seal Cutter's Mis-fortune" ANTIQUITY, Vol. LI., No. 1., March 1977

During Caspers, Dr. Elisabeth C.L. "A Short Survey of a Still Topical Problem: The Third Millennium Arabian Gulf Trade Mechanism Seen in the Light of the Recent Discoveries in Southern Iran" ACTA PRAEHISTORIA ET ARCHAEOLOGICA, Sonderdruck, 3. 1972

During Caspers, Dr. Elisabeth C.L. "The Bahrain Tumuli" (A Summary of the paper read at the Proceedings of the 5th Seminar for Arabian Studies, held at the Oriental Institute, Oxford, 22nd/.23rd September 1971) INSTITUTE OF ARCHAEOLOGY (London) 1972

During Caspers, Dr. Elisabeth C.L. "The Bahrain Tumuli: An Illustrated Catalogue of Two Important Collections" NEDERLANDS HISTORISCH-ARCHAEOLOGISCH INSTITUT TE ISTANBUL, 1980

During Caspers, Dr. Elisabeth C.L. "The Bull's Hpad from Barbaŕ Temple II, Bahrain. A Contact with early Dynastic Sumer" EAST AND WEST (New Series) Vol. 21, Nos. 3-4, Sept.-Dec. 1971, Is. MEO (Rome)

During Caspers, Dr. Elisabeth C.L. "Harappan Trade in the Arabian Gulf in the 3rd Millennium B.C." (A Short Digest of the Paper read to the B.H.A.S. on 5th March 1973 DILMUN, No. 5, December 1973

During Caspers, Dr. Elisabeth C.L. "Statuary in the Round from Dilmun" PROCEEDINGS FOR ARABIAN STUDIES, INSTITUTE OF ARCHAEOLOGY (London), Vol. 6., 1976

El-Said, Issam, Ayse Parman, GEOMETRIC CONCEPTS IN ISLAMIC ART, World of Islarn Festival Publishing Co. Ltd. (London) 1976

Fisher, Prof. W.B. THE MIDDLE EAST: A PHYSICAL, SOCIAL AND REGIONAL GEOGRAPHY, Methuen and Co. (London) 7th ed. 1978

Fleming, John, Hugh Honour, Nikolaus Pevsner THE PENGUIN DICTIONARY OF ARCHITECTURE Penguin Books Ltd. (London) 2nd ed. 1972

Frings, Mary "Dutch to build Bahrain Causeway", FINANCIAL TIMES 9th July 1981

Frings, Mary "New Causeway island to House Cement Plant" GULF MIRROR, 11th-17th July 1981, p.2

Ghaidam, Usam "A Sense of Place at the Market" GULF TIMES, 6th 12th July 1980, p. 24

Ghaidam, Usam "How Windtowers Benefit Designers" GULF TIMES, 29th June - 5th July 1980, p. 24

262

Glob, P.V. "The Flint Sites of the Bahrain Desert" KUML, 1954, pp. 112-131

Glob, P.V. "Temples at Barbar" KUML, 1954, pp. 150-160

Hardy-Guilbert, Claire, Christian Lalande, "La Maison de Shaykh Isa a Bahrayn" Recherche sur les Grandes Civilisations, Memoire No. 8. Histoire du Golfe, Editions A.D.P.F. (Paris) with English translation

Hawkins, C.W. THE DHOW Nautical Publishing Co. Ltd., Lymington Hampshire (UK) 1977

Howarth, Lt. Cdr. David DHOWS Quartet Books Ltd. (London) 1977

Ibrahim, Dr. Moawiyah "Abstracts from an address given to the B.H. A.S. on Excavations at Diraz, Saar and Barbar", 20.6.81, B.H.A.S. Library.

India Office Library and Records, Ref. R/15/2/1771 "Description of the Al-Khamis Mosque, Bilad Al-Qadim"

Izzard, Molly THE GULF: ARABIA'S WESTERN APPROACHES John Murray (London) 1979

Kanoo, Dr. Abdul Latif "Ornamentation and Decoration found in early systems of Construction of Arabia" DILMUN, Winter, 1974/5

Keating, Aileen "The Shopping Centre where you can't see the Hood for the Trees" KHALEEJ TIMES MAGAZINE, 6th March 1981, No. 115, pp. 28-9

Kernahan, Anne "Golden Future for Bahrain" GULF MIRROR, 2nd-8th August, 1980

Khunji, Farida Moh. Saleh THE STORY OF THE PALM TREE (adapted for English readers by J.R. Simpson) Ministry of Information, Bahrain

Khuri, Fuad I. TRIBE AND STATE IN BAHRAIN: THE TRANS-FORMATION OF SOCIAL AND POLITICAL AUTHORITY IN AN ARAB STATE University of Chicago, Published by the Center for Middle Eastern Studies, Number 14, 1980

Kozack, Peter A. (Ed.) "Bahrain - A Half Century of Oil, Partnership and Progress" OIL LIFESTREAM OF PROGRESS, Number One, 1980, pp. 2-9 (Published by Caltex)

Kozack, Peter A. (Ed.) "Bahrain - Crossroads of the Middle East" OIL LIFESTREAM OF PROGRESS Vol. 26, No. 2, 1976 pp. 2-9

Lalande, Christian REPORT MISSION ARCHEOLOGIQUE FRAN-
CAISE U.N.E.S.C.O. Ministere Francais des Affaires Etrangeres;
Ministere de l'education de l'etat de Bahrain

Lane Fox, Robin THE SEARCH FOR ALEXANDER Allen Lane
(London) 1980

Lewcock, Prof. Ronald BAHRAIN CONSULTANT REPORT: Conservation, Restoration and Presentation of Monuments of Archaeological Sites of the Islamic Period (Reports 1 and 2) U.N.E.S.C.O.
1979

Lewis, Prof. Bernard (Ed) THE WORLD OF ISLAM Thames and
Hudson (London) 1976

LLoyd, Seton THE ARCHAEOLOGY OF MESOPOTAMIA FROM
THE OLD STONE AGE TO THE PERSIAN CONQUEST Thames
and Hudson (London) 1978

Mackay, Ernest J.H. (with Lankester Harding, Sir Flinders Petrie)
"1925 Bahrain and Hemamieh" Publications of British School of
Archaeology in Egypt, University College, London BERNARD
QUARITCH (London) 1929

Maloney, Joan, Shirley Kay (Eds.) ANTIQUITIES OF BAHRAIN:
A GUIDE TO THE ANCIENT SITES OF BAHRAIN, B.H.A.S.,
in co-operation with the Antiquities Division of the Bahrain
Education Department 1970.

McNicholl, Dr. A.W. "Al-Markh excavations" sponsored by the
Committee for Arabian and Gulf Studies PROCEEDINGS OF
THE SEMINAR FOR ARABIAN STUDIES, Vol. 6, 1976 INSTI-
TUTE OF ARCHAEOLOGY (London) 1976

McNicholl, Dr. A.W. "Al-Markh, Diraz and Janusan: An address Given
to the B.H.A.S. 6th February 1974, B.H.A.S. Library

Rice, M. "The Grave Complex at Al-Hajjar Bahrain" Preliminary Report
PROCEEDINGS OF THE 5TH SEMINAR FOR ARABIAN
STUDIES held at the Oriental Institute, Oxford 22nd/23rd
September 1971 pp. 66-75

Pelly, Lt. Col. L. "Remarks on the Oyster Beds in the Persian Gulf"
ROYAL ASIATIC SOCIETY, 1868

Petocz, Dani, Stephen Hart "Report of the Australian Team Working
for the Bahrain Department of Antiquities" B.H.A.S. Library
1979-80

Porada, Prof. Edith "Remarks on Seals Found in the Gulf States"
3rd International Conference on Asian Archaeology in Bahrain,
March 1970 ARTIBUS ASIAE, Vol. XXXIII, 4, 1971, Institute
of Fine Arts, New York University

Prideaux, Col. F.B. "The Sepulchral Tumuli of Bahrain" ARCHAEO-LOGICAL SURVEY OF INDIA - ANNUAL REPORT, 1908-9, pp. 60-78

Ruffle, John (Ed.) OMAN AND THE SINDABAD PROJECT: The Record of an Exhibition at the Gulbenkian Museum, Durham, from November 1980 to February 1981, The Gulbenkian Museum of Oriental Art, University of Durham, 1980

Safadi, Y.H. ISLAMIC CALLIGRAPHY Thames and Hudson (London) 1978

Scott, John S. THE PENGUIN DICTIONARY OF CIVIL ENGINEER-ING Penguin Books Ltd. (London) 1980, 3rd. ed.

Seymour, Ian "The Oil Scene in Bahrain" MIDDLE EAST ECONOMIC SURVEY, Vol. XXIV, No. 35, 15.6.81, pp. 12-14

Stegner, Wallace DISCOVERY: THE SEARCH FOR ARABIAN OIL Middle East Export Press Inc. (Lebanon) 1971

Wallace, Jonathan "Gulf University Gets the Green Light" MIDDLE EAST ECONOMIC DIGEST, 22nd May 1981, Vo. 25, No. 21 p. 6

Whelan, John "The Gulf Council: An Exercise in Collaboration and Co-operation" MIDDLE EAST ECONOMIC DIGEST, 29th May 1981, Vol. 25, No 22, p.2

Whitten, D.G.A. (with J.R.V. Brooks) THE PENGUIN DICTIONARY OF GEOLOGY Penguin Books (London) 1972

Williams, Jean "Tunnels Lead to the Past" GULF MIRROR 20th-26th December 1980, p. 11

Wright, G.R.H. THE OLD AMIRI PALACE, DOHA, QATAR Institut Francais d'Archeologie, Beirut, Qatar National Museum 1975

Zayani, Shaoki "Project Unique to Islam" GULF MIRROR' 6th-12th June 1981, p. 7

Sandars, N.K. THE EPIC OF GILGAMESH: An English Version with an Introduction, Penguin Books (London) 1960; revised 1972; re-printed 1981

ZIYADEH, Dr. Nicola "History of the Arabian Gulf" Notes on a talk given to the B.H.A.S., DILMUN, No. 2 June 1972

Newspaper Sources

ARAB NEWS, "Gulf University will accommodate 10,000 students" 26.6.81; "Bridge to boost Bahrain Economy" 9.7.81

ARAB TIMES, "Bahrain Emerging as World Bullion Centre" 20.11.80; "A Causeway to link all Gulf States" 9.7.81; "Gulf Council Heading for Unified Monetary System" 8.8.81; "Gulf Council: a Move towards Self-Reliance" 14.7.81

FINANCIAL TIMES, "Record Results for OBUs in Bahrain" 7.5.81

GULF BANKING & FINANCE MAGAZINE "Bahrain as major Gold Market" April 1981 No. 4 pp 3-7

GULF DAILY NEWS, "OBUs show a healthy profit" 6.5.81; "Census Results" 27.4.81; "6-year target òf new University" 28.6.81; "BD 2m. Lifeline to Fishermen" 24.8.81; "Causeway gets the final seal" 9.7.81/10.7.81; "Island Plans a Major Drive for tourists" 21.7.81

GULF MIRROR, "Block ready by the end of 1982" 11.7.81; "GCC Agrees on Common Currency" 11.7.81; "Determined to End a 10-year Power Vacuum" 30.5.81; "New Life for Old Palace" 26.7.81

GULF TIMES, "Golden Prospects for Bahrain" 30.11.80

KHALEEJ TIMES, "Plans to Develop Bahrain Airport" 21.5.81; "New Departure Terminal for Bahrain Airport" 5.81; "One more OBU for Bahrain" 13.2.81; "Digging Up the Past in Bahrain" 14.5.81; "Bahrain OBUs improve earning 50%" 14.7.81; Bahrain-Saudi Causeway Pact Signed" 9.7.81

MIDDLE EAST ECONOMIC SURVEY, "Bahrain Moves to Control Gold Market" 20.4.81 No. 27, p. III

Other Sources

BAHRAIN CURRENCY BOARD - Annual Reports 1966-1974

BAHRAIN MONETARY AGENCY - Annual Reports 1975-1979

BAHRAIN OFFICIAL GAZETTE (English Translation) Issue No. 1445, 23.7.81 Amiri Decree No. 8 of 1981 with respect to establishing new directorates at the Ministry of Information

BAPCO Annual Report 1967 "Traffic Change"

PRIVATE INFORMATION CENTRE ON EASTERN ARABIA Heldenplein 12, 1800 Vilvoorde, Belgium "Fact Sheets on Eastern Arabia: History, Bahrain" Date: May 1973 Ref. F/C/1

CHRONOLOGY

c. 6,000 B.C.	Bahrain ceases to be connected to the mainland
c. 3,800 B.C.	State of Dilmun thought to have been established
c. 2,000 B.C.	Dilmun's importance begins to decline
	Indo-European tribes called Aryans invade present-day Pakistan and destroy Indus Valley civilisation
750 B.C.	Assyrian Kings claim sovereignty over the islands from this date
c. 600 B.C.	Bahrain incorporated into Babylonian Empire
c. 540 B.C.	Persians conquer Bahrain
c. 300 B.C.	Bahrain incorporated into the Seleucid Dynasty
0-300 A.D.	Parthian Period
4th cent.	Shappur II, Sassanian King, annexes Bahrain
7th-11th cents.	Bahrain ruled by governors on behalf of the Caliphs of Damascus and Baghdad
1058	Abu-l-Bahlul, one of Bahrain's leading inhabitants, revolted against Carmathian rule and proclaimed himself prince
15th cent.	Bahrain united with Qatif and Hasa under Sh. Ibrahim Al-Maliki
1487	Omani invasion and the appointment of Umar bin Al-Khattab as governor
1510	Portuguese capture Goa; expansion towards Hormuz
1521	Islands fall into Portuguese hands after which Bahrain Fort was built
1560	Long conflict between Turkey and the Portuguese empire over control of the Arabian Gulf ends
1602	Bahrain ceases to be a vassal to Hormuz and the Portuguese
1645	Portuguese send a fleet from India to destroy Hormuz and Bahrain

267

1720	Persians purchase Bahrain from the Omanis
c. 1747	Khalifa dies.
	Muhammad bin Khalifa migrates to Zubara
1776	Muhammad bin Khalifa dies, succeeded by his son, Khalifa bin Muhammad
1782	Khalifa bin Muhammad dies, succeeded by Ahmed Al-Fatih (The Conqueror)
1783	Ahmed Al-Fatih captures Bahrain
1796	Ahmed Al-Fatih dies, succeeded by his sons Sulman and Abdulla as Joint Rulers
c. 1800	Arad Fort built by the Omanis
	Sulman retires to Zubara, Qatar
1820	Sulman returns to Bahrain
1825	Sulman dies, succeeded by his son Khalifa, as Joint Ruler with Abdulla
1834	Khalifa bin Sulman dies leaving Abdulla as sole ruler
c. 1840	Abu Mahur Fort built
1843	Abdulla deposed, besieged in Abu Mahur Fort and exiled by Muhammad bin Khalifa
1848	Abdulla dies in exile in Saudi Arabia
1861	Treaty of Peace and Friendship signed with Britain
1864	Muhammad bin Abdulla attempts to seize Bahrain
1868	Muhammad bin Khalifa fled to Qatar
1869	Muhammad bin Khalifa invaded Bahrain, killed his brother Ali, re-instated himself as Ruler, was deposed and held captive by cousin Muhammad bin Abdulla, and deported by the British together with his cousin
	Isa, grandson of Khalifa bin Sulman, re-called from exile in Qatar by the British, proclaimed Ruler of Bahrain

1902	American Mission Hospital opened
1909	Quarantine Station built
1912	Maritime Port of Manama (Mina Manama) built with a goods warehouse
1923	Sh. Isa abdicates in favour of his son
1925	Eastern and General Syndicate granted a two-year oil-prospecting concession by H.H. the late Shaikh Hamed bin Isa Al-Khalifa, 2nd December
1926	Oil concession rejected by the British Government
	First surfaced road on the island built between Jebel Camp and Awali
1927	The Eastern Gulf Company acquire a two-year oil-prospecting option from Eastern and General syndicate
	Ralph Rhoades arrives in Bahrain to map the island on behalf of Eastern Gulf Oil Co.
1928	Standard Oil Company of California (SOCAL) buys Bahrain option from Gulf Oil Corporation, 27th December
	Rhoades reports on his field-work conducted between 6th February and 19th March
	Major Frank Holmes had drilled 35 water wells
	Standard Oil Company of California (SOCAL) adopts Bahrain interests in the Gulf, 21st December
1929	Bahrain Petroleum Company Ltd. (BAPCO) incorporated in Canada, as a fully-owned subsidiary of Standard Oil of California, 11th January
	Power House, providing electricity to Manama, became operational to provide electricity for "2000 lamps and 200 fans"
1930	Fred A. Davies marks the site for drilling
	Work began on the Sh. Hamed Causeway
	Eastern and General Syndicate formally assigned its rights to BAPCO, 1st August

	Small experimental garden set up in Budaiya
1931	The power supply extended to Muharraq
	Bahrain's first oil well "spudded in", 16th October
1932	Oil flows on the 1st June
	Telephone system installed, 12 lines and one public telephone
	First Imperial Airways machine landed in Bahrain en route to India on the Manama race-course, 1st October
	Shaikh Isa dies on 9th December
	Oil Well No. 2 flows, Christmas Day
1934	First shipment of crude leaves Bahrain in SOCAL tanker El Sequndo, 6th June
	First houses constructed in Awali
	13 oil wells producing crude
	Sh. Hamed (grandfather of the present Amir) granted BAPCO a mining lease, 29th December
1935	Work started on the construction of the refinery
1936	First refinery unit completed in summer with a capacity of approximately 10,000 b.p.d.
	Sh. Hamed created Honorary Knight Commander of the Order of the Indian Empire (KCIE)
	CALTEX incorporated, June
	Sh. Hamed Causeway opened to road traffic
1937	Jebel Camp vacated
1938	Awali officially named
	Friday Mosque built with first oil revenues
	First petrol filling-station opened
1939	Air-conditioners introduced into Manama
1940	Work commences on the swing-bridge spanning the

	deep-water channel connecting the two ends of Muharraq-Manama Causeway
1942	Muharraq-Manama Causeway completed with the completion of the swing-bridge
	Shaikh Hamed dies, succeeded by Shaikh Sulman
1944	Old Sitra Pier ceased to be used.
1950	Gulf Aviation Company was formed, a project which owed its inception to an ex-RAF Officer, Frederick Bosworth
1953	Bahrain Historical and Archaeological Society founded
	Gregorian calendar replaces the Arabic calendar for official budgets and accounts
	Mahooz Power Station completed
1955	Bahrain Broadcasting Station (BBS) came "on air" in August
1956	Bait Skinner demolished
	Edward Skinner dies in New York, aged 64
	Sir Charles Belgrave, the Ruler's Adviser, retires
1957	First Bahrain Agricultural Show
1959	Fred A. Davies retires as Chairman of the Board of Directors of ARAMCO, visits Bahrain on a farewell trip
	New airport terminal at Muharraq
	Swing-bridge still operational
1960	Sh. Sulman lays foundation stone for the new air-port building
	"Free Transit" area formed at Mina Sulman
	7,000 cars on the island
1961	H.H. Sh. Sulman bin Hamed Al-Khalifa dies, succeeded by H.H. Shaikh Isa bin Sulman Al-Khalifa, the present Amir, 2nd November

	Accession ceremony, 16th December
1964	Bahrain Currency Board formed
1965	Currency changed from Indian External Rupee to Bahrain dinar, October
1967	Mina Sulman, named after the late Ruler, came into operation
1968	Bahrain Defence Force formed
	Isa Town project inaugurated
	Earth Satellite station installed
	Delmon Hotel built, the first international hotel in Bahrain
1969	Earth Station at Ras Abu Jarjur opened
1970	Work starts on new airport
	3rd International Asian Archaeology Conference ce
	Bahrain Museum opened
1971	Bahrain's First National Day
	New airport officially opened
	Declaration of Independence, 14th August
	Bahrain admitted to the United Nations as 128th member
	New Treaty of Friendship signed with Britiain, 15th August
	Public bus service came into operation
	New airport terminal opened specifically designed for "Jumbo" jets
1973	Bahrain admitted to the League of Arab States
1974	Bahrain Monetary Agency formed
	Work began on the dry dock, built under the auspices of the Organisation of Arab Petroleum Exporting Countries (OAPEC)

1975	Construction starts on new Sitra Power Station
1976	Concorde arrives in Bahrain, 21st January
1977	Bahrain-Sitra causeway completed
	Palace of the Heir Apparent, H.E. Shaikh Hamed bin Isa Al-Khalifa completed
	Arab Shipbuilding and Repair Yard (ASRY) officially opened its $340 million dry-dock complex, financed by OAPEC, 15th December
	Bahrain National Oil Company (BANOCO) formed
1978	Mina Sulman container terminal completed
	Central Market completed
1979	Initialling of Participation Agreement between the government and BAPCO
1980	Enforcement of Hallmarking Law
1981	The Amir opens the new racecourse, March
	National census results published. Population: 358,857, 27th April
	Signing of Bahrain-Saudi Arabia Causeway Contract, 8th July
	First Summit Meeting held of the Gulf Co-operation Council in Abu Dhabi, 25th May
	New Directorate of Heritage and Directorate of Tourism created under the Ministry of Information; Directorate of Museums and Archaeology transferred from Ministry of Education to Ministry of Information, 20th August

273

GLOSSARY

ABBAH (abbaya). Black covering worn over a women's dress and head for purposes of Islamic modesty when in public

ABBAYA (see (Abbah)

ABU. Father

ADHARI. Virgin (Hence: Adhari Pool or Ain Adhari)

ADZE. Axe-like tool with arched blade at right-angles to the handle

AIN (Ayn). Fresh-water spring

AL. The

AL-GHAWS. Diving Season

AL-RAKBA. Opening day of the diving season

AQUIFER. Water-bearing bed of stratified rocks by virtue of their porosity (see also Artesian structure).

ARTESIAN STRUCTURE. A series of sedimentary rocks aligned in such a way that an aquifer holds water under a pressure-head between two layers of impermeable strata. When a well is sunk into the aquifer, water rises.to the surface by virtue of the pressure-head.

ASEEL. Grass grown between the sweet spring water and the seashore.

AWAL. Idol.

AWALI. High Place.

AYN (see ain).

BAB. Gateway (Hence: Bab Al-Bahrain)

BADGEER (see badgir)

BADGIR (BADGEER). Aeration system obtained by the particular type of opening in the walls of a room, especially in the upper register at sub-roof level.

BAGHLEH. Two-handled storage jar usually for water.

BAHRAIN. Two seas. (c/f Ain i.e. Bahr-ain)

BAIT (Bayt). House

274

BARASTI. Palm-frond shelter or house

BASTION. A projection at an angle of a fortification, from which the garrison can see and defend the ground before the ramparts.

BAYT (see bait).

BIAMAHAB. Sea-bed fresh water source.

BILAD AL-QADIM. Old Town

BIN. son of

BISHT. Formal, light-weight woollen cloak worn by men. Usually black or dark brown and embroidered with gold thread round the edges, worn over a dishdasha or thobe.

BOOM. Large ocean-going passenger and cargo vessel between 40-100 metres long (131-328 feet).

CALLIGRAPHY. Decorative handwriting, esp. in Korans.

CHISEH. Container for carrying birds and poultry made from asig (palm-tree stalk on which the dates grow)

CORNICE. Projecting ornamental moulding along the top of a building wall or arch.

CRENELLATION. Parapet with alternating indentations and raised portions; also called merlon or battlement.

DANCHE. Mangrove poles often treated with bitumen to provide wooden frames for roof-matting (see jareed).

DARISHA. Unglazed window casements in the lower register of a wall.

DATSHA. Masonry bench for sitting on outside, usually at the entrance to a room, or along the length of a wall.

DEHYEEN. Bag for collecting oysters.

DHOW. A traditional wooden sailing craft, associated with the Arabian Gulf and the Indian Ocean. Now most vessels are powered by engines.

DIHLIZ. Entrance or vestibule.

DISHDASHA. Long cotton robe, worn by Arabian men. Usually open-necked. Colour variations and tailoring designs reveal much about the wearer's social and geographic background.

275

DIWAN. Reception room of palace or large private house.

DJIBSIN (see gypsum).

DJISS (see gypsum).

DUKHAN. Smoke. (Hence: Jebel Dukhan - Mountain of Smoke)

DYKE. Water channel with an earth embankment, usually employed for irrigation purposes.

FAROUSH. Sea coral aggregate used as a building material.

FARSH. Stones from the regular strata of Bahrain island's bedrock. Cut into slabs, these stones are used for the bays of wall masonry and for internal partition walls, viz: houses and tumuli chambers.

FOOTA'AM. Divers' nose pinchers/clips.

GARGOYLE. Water spout projecting from a roof or the parapet of a wall or tower, usually carved into a figure.

GA'WA (gahwah). Coffee-house where Arabian men congregate and smoke gidu (water-pipes).

GAHWAH (see ga'wa).

GEMINATED ARCHES. Double arches, arranged in pairs.

GIDU. Water-pipe or "hubbly-bubbly".

GYPSUM (djiss, djibsin, jus, juss). Limestone based on pulverised and burnt gypsum that provides powder to make plaster and the mortar used for masonry work. Used because of its quick-setting properties.

HADJAR AL-BAHR. Sea-stone, coral aggregate blocks, formed by coalescence of crystallized carbonate of lime. It provides a very strong building stone, but its high salt content renders it difficult to use.

HADRA. Wooden fish-traps made from palm-reeds.

HALAT. Hamlet.

HAMMAM. Public baths.

HASA. Rubble.

HAWSH. Inner court of house.

HOWAR. Young camel. (Hence: Howar Islands)

HYPOSTYLE. A hall or other large space over which the roof is supported by rows of columns giving a forest-like appearance.

IBN. Son of.

IMAM. Leader of the Moslem congregation.

ITHIL. Wooden poles of tamarisk.

JABAL (see jebel).

JALIBUT. Coastal trading vessel, originally used for pearl-diving and distinguished by a vertical stem. Length varies between 15 and 30 metres (49 and 99 feet).

JAREED. Roof-matting made from palm leaves.

JAZEERA (see jazira).

JAZIRA (jazeera). Island.

JEBEL (jabal). Mountain or hill (Hence: Jebel Dukhan).

JEBEL DUKHAN. Mountain of Smoke. A range which rises to 122.4 metres in the centre of Bahrain island.

JIRBEH. Goat-skin water bag.

JUS (see gypsum).

JUSS (see gypsum).

KHABAT. Divers' finger guards.

KHALEEJ (khalij). Gulf. (Hence: Khaleej Times)

KHALIJ (see khaleej).

KHANAT (see qanat).

KHAWR (see khor).

KHOR (khawr). Bay or creek.

KHUFF. Camel's footprint.

KIBLA (see qibla).

KRUM. Red wood imported from Java, used for window shutters, esp. Bait Sh. Isa.

LIWAN. Portico., wide-open on one side, for resting in or where tea was served.

MADEH. Reed mat woven from aseel grass grown between the sweet and salt water line, especially on Nabih Salih and Sitra islands.

MADJLIS (see majlis).

MADRASAH. School.

MAGHZAN. Secondary majlis (reception room).

MAJLIS (madjlis). Reception room in an Arab home, also a public reception hosted by a noteable.

MANAMA. Place of sleeping.

MANGROVE. Timber used for pillars or beams for the flooring and roofing of house and palace architecture. Imported from India. Exceptionally durable as a building material.

MANKUR. Woven palm frond matting, covered with masonry, used as floor or roof stiffening.

MARZAM. Wooden gargoyle.

MASKAR. Fish-trap.

MATAM. Two wings of a fish-trap. (see Hadra).

MERLON (see crenellation).

MESHABEH. Woven palm-frond fan for kitchen fires.

MIDDEN. Refuse heap.

MIHAFFA. Woven palm face-fan.

MIHRAB. A niche in the wall indicating the direction of Mecca.

MIMBAR. Elevated pulpit in a mosque.

MINA. Port.

MUEZZIN. Official of a mosque who proclaims prayer times from the minaret.

MUHARRAQ. Place of burning. Originally the name was attributed to a place on the island of the same name where the Hindu cremated their deceased.

MURAQIB. Local name for the tumuli or burial mounds.

MUSALA AL-ARISH. Porch or covered terrace with a dried branch canopy.

NAKHUDA. The master of a dhow.

NAQSHA. Stucco screens in the upper register of a wall.

NURA. Lime, especially for the use of whitewash.

QA. Arabic transliteration rarely follows the English convention of the vowel 'u' following the letter 'q'. Most Arabic words which begin with this letter are followed by vowels a or i in transliteration.

QADIL. Deepwater dip where the fish are caught in a hadra (fish-trap).

QALAAT (qala'at). Fort. (Hence: Qalaat Al-Bahrain).

QANAT (khanat). Underground system of conduits used for irrigation.

QASAB. Matting.

QIBLA (kibla). The direction of prayer to Mecca. Hence mosques are built in alignment to the qibla.

QUERN. Wheel-shaped stone slab which is rotated by hand over a similarly shaped piece of stone, between which corn is placed for grinding.

RAS. Headland.

RAS RUMMAAN. Headland of Pomegranates.

RASSAMIN. Specialised fishermen who make fish-traps.

RAWSHINA. Middle register of recesses in a wall.

RIFAA AL-GHARBI. West Rifaa town.

RIFAA AL-SHARQI. East Rifaa town.

RUSHANA. Decorative and functional niche, set in the walls of a room.

SABOG. Large woven dish for dates.

SAHN. Courtyard where the fountain for ablution is located.

SALEH. Clothes basket.

SALEH RUTAB. Woven container with lid, for storing dates.

SAMBUK. Wooden vessel used mostly for sardine fishing and pearl-diving expeditions. Length varies between 15-20 metres (49-66 feet); ocean-going over 40 metres long (131 feet).

SH. Abbreviation of Shaikh (Sheikh).

SHU'AI. Wooden coastal vessel for local transport and fishing up to 50 metres long (164 feet).

SKIFF. Small light boat, esp. for rowing or sculling.

SOFFIT. The underside of any architectural element.

SOFRAH. Woven floor dining mat for displaying food dishes.

SONDAGE. Test shaft or sounding used in archaeological investigations.

SOUK (see suq).

SOUQ (see suq).

STEATITE. Soapstone.

SUQ (souk, souq). Market.

SUQ AL-KHAMIS. Thursday Market.

SUZERAIN. Feudal overlord. A state or sovereign exercising some degree of dominion over a dependent state, usually controlling its foreign affairs.

TANNUR. Fireplace.

THAUB (see thobe).

THOBE (thaub). A man's long dress or shift garment, usually buttoned to the neck. Often white, it may be made in pastel colours such as cream, pale blue, pale green or grey. Braiding or some kind of border may be applied for formal wear, especially when a bisht (woollen cloak) is worn as an over-garment.

THOBE AL-NASHEL. A lady's long festive dress with gold embroidery.

TRAPEZOID. Quadrilateral figure, area or ground-plan where no sides are parallel.

TREFOIL. Lobe or leaf-shaped curve formed by the cusping of a circle or an arch.

UBAID CULTURE. Named after its type-site located on the Euphrates River in Southern Iraq. Pottery of this culture has been excavated in Bahrain.

UMM. Mother.

UMM AL-HASSAM. Mother of Pebbles. Used figuratively to connote abundance.

UMM AL-KHAYLEH. Mother of the small palm tree.

WADI. Intermittent watercourse in semi-desert areas.

WEZIR (wazir, vezir (Turkish), Vizier (Venetian). A high official in certain Moslem countries, who served in various capacities such as that of provincial governor or Chief Minister to the Sultan, esp. Oman.

YAD. The 'hand' or centre of a fish-trap (hadra).

YADHAW. Palm trunks used in masonry as supporting and connecting joists for the flooring and roofing in traditional Arabian Gulf architecture.

SITE INDEX

SHAIKH ABDULAZIZ BIN MOHAMMED
AL KHALIFA
1932-1981

The Bahrain Historical & Archaeological Society wishes to express its great regret at the untimely death of the late Shaikh Abdulaziz, who was one of the founding members of the newly revitalized society in 1970, its president from 1970-1973 and one of the few honorary members of the society. Shaikh Abdulaziz was with the Ministry of Education from 1959 and was Minister from 1972 until his premature death earlier this year. We are deeply indebted to him for all his past support and his death is a sad loss to all.

ABOUT THE AUTHOR

Angela Clarke spent the early years of her career working for the BBC World Service in London, prior to an assignment to the archaeology and history television series "Chronicle". In 1973 she graduated from the University of Birmingham (UK) in History and Archaeology and returned to the British Broadcasting Corporation to pursue radio and television research. In her spare time she edited "Archaeolog" the magazine of the Archaeological Group of the Royal Photographic Society in England. Since arriving in Bahrain 3 years ago the author has been a member of the Bahrain Historical and Archaeological Society, the publishers of this Guide.

NOTES